WINGD

Presents

An Insider's Guide to Canada's Capital

ISBN 978-1-77216-096-3

Published by:
Baico Publishing Consultants Inc.
Suite 402 - 280 Albert Street,
Ottawa, Ontario. K1P 5G8
Phone: 613-829-5141
Fax: 613-829-5152
info@baico.ca
www.baico.ca

Printed by:
Du Progrès Printing
Unit 5 - 171 Jean-Proulx Street,
Gatineau, Quebec. J8Z 1W5
Phone: 819-778-2122
info@duprogres.ca
www.duprogres.ca

CONTENTS

We are very excited to share a piece of our city, Ottawa, with everyone. It has taken us two years to create this guidebook about our Nation's Capital and we are so proud to finally see our hard work come to fruition. Ottawa is often perceived as a boring city that lacks creativity but we do not think that way. We hope that this book will help the true nature of Ottawa shine forth, unburdened by negative stereotypes. Ottawa is an amazing city and we are honoured to call it our home.

- *The Wingd Team*

1

Mayor Jim Watson. Photography by Rebecca Hay

FOREWORD

As mayor of Canada's National Capital, I am thrilled to have the opportunity to introduce this book to you. In the past, Ottawa was thought of as being a boring city. As mayor of this city that would make me a #BoringMayor. However, I've been known to attend several community events, and proclaim as many days as there are stars in the sky. My perceived omnipresence has inspired cartoonists to depict me cloning myself. Some people even joke that I show up at the opening of an envelope. But what I have learned from helping new business owners inaugurate their stores, talking to kids and students about civic engagement, and visiting attractions across the city, is that every person and place in Ottawa has a story worth telling.

Several things set Ottawa apart, some of which include, its large geographical scale, the presence of nationally ranked universities and colleges, as well as the presence of eight of the ten national museums of Canada and dozens of local museums, galleries and historical sites, the Rideau Canal, multiple festivals and fairs hosted by our rural communities, our enviable food scene, and the openness of our Parliament Buildings for free guided tours and school excursions.

As I write this, Ottawa is at the pinnacle of an economic, infrastructural, and cultural boom. The entire country is getting ready to celebrate the 150th anniversary of Canada's Confederation, right here in Ottawa. The year 2017 will mark a historical time in the Nation's Capital's history, and we will showcase to the world that Ottawa is a world class city. The legacy that #Ottawa2017 will leave for its residents, tourists, and visitors will be enjoyed and treasured for many years to come.

Like me, many folks came to Ottawa to study and remained after their studies because they fall in love with this city. In fact, that's what the authors of this book have done, and through this literary and photographic experience, you will see why amongst so many others, they have chosen to plant their roots here.

BECOMING WINGD

Written by Zainab N. Muse & David Ebere,
Co-founders of Wingd

The intention of Wingd has always been to squash negative perceptions of millennials as uncreative and unmotivated people. We launched Wingd in order to provide opportunities for people to communicate relevant content in a world where superficial information often makes the rounds. Oftentimes, media platforms put a spotlight on people and things that don't directly affect our lives intrinsically. So, Wingd was created to refocus people's attention on to things that do matter, like extraordinary people living in seemingly ordinary times. Gradually, as Wingd took shape, we created a digital multimedia platform that comprises of several independent ventures. Some of these ventures include an award-winning blogging platform that promotes positive journalism, our millennial entrepreneur-centered podcast, documentary style videos highlighting global innovation and a nonprofit branch that facilitates global campaigns that promote youth collaboration to solve some of the world's toughest problems. Once the digital platform was established, we decided to shift into print with our first book. Our next print project is a magazine series.

Our first book is a guidebook on Canada's National Capital Region (NCR) with a hyper focus on Ottawa. It aims to explore the microcosm in which the Wingd team was formed. We are currently a team of more than two dozen people and the assembly of this book required all of our members, as well as some additional freelancers. Our team consists of amazingly talented writers, photographers, graphic designers and videographers. We are extremely thankful for the team's dedication to this project.

This guidebook was an incredible accomplishment that took us two years to complete and we couldn't be more proud to share part of the product of our hard work with you. We once heard that Ottawa is a city that lacks creativity, and it was this casual observation that fuelled our ambition to create our book. Although, we are both originally from Nigeria, we quickly started to call Ottawa, 'home'. Please, turn the page, and share in our perspective of our beloved city; you'll never think of Ottawa as boring again.

the wingd team.

Left to Right; Top - Daniel Effah, Sarah Khalid, Boris Nzaramba, Felixe Denson, Lorietta Muse, Claire Leunissen, Julia Weber, Jenna Sheikh, Rebecca Hay, Richard E. Gower, David Ebere, Zainab N. Muse, and Michael Tang. Bottom - Syed Zeehad, Shuyi Yang, Rachelle Bélanger, Sam Lehman, Soumi Ghosh, Navita Patel, and Jimmy Lau. **Missing in Photo**: Tony Li, Gloria Charles-Pierre, John Lin, Orphane Beaulière, Amulya Gururaj, Paroma Datta, Noorulabdeen Ahmad, and Anjali Ramburn.

Photography by Jenna Sheikh

DEFINITIONS

Canada's Capital: Canada's capital city, refers to the city of Ottawa in the province of Ontario.

Confederation Boulevard: This is the Capital's ceremonial and discovery route. It runs a length of 7.5 kilometres and forms a loop that connects both sides of the Ottawa River linking Ontario and Quebec, predominantly the downtown areas of Ottawa and Gatineau. It connects many sites of national significance like Parliament Hill and the Supreme Court of Canada, as well as museums, heritage sites, embassies, monuments, parks, pathways and beautiful natural landscapes.

Confederation Park: This site is a major feature of Confederation Boulevard. It was opened in 1967 and is about 2.63 hectares in size. The park also features several monuments, sculptures and a memorial fountain honouring Lieutenant-Colonel John By.

Confederation Square: This is a National Historic Site of Canada located in Downtown Ottawa. The area is roughly triangular in shape and it is framed by landmark buildings, some of which include the Fairmont Château Laurier, the National Arts Centre, and the Parliamentary East Block. In addition, the National War Memorial sits at the Square's centre.

National Capital Greenbelt: This is a band of green space commissioned by the National Capital Commission / Commission de la capitale nationale (NCC/CCN) that spans Ottawa from west to east. It includes several wetlands, farms, sand dunes, and streams that sustain biodiversity.

National Capital Region (NCR): Also known as Canada's Capital Region, refers to the official designation for Ottawa, Gatineau and their surrounding urban and rural communities. Thus, the Capital Region includes the Ottawa-Gatineau area.

Ottawa 2017: An epic, year-long celebration of the 150th anniversary of Canada, commissioned to take place in Ottawa throughout 2017.

Ottawan: Someone who lives or was born and raised in the city of Ottawa.

MEMORY LANE

Ottawa was once called Bytown. The name came about as an homage to Lieutenant-Colonel John By of the Royal Engineers, who landed in the area, along with his engineering staff in 1826. The engineers arrived with the intention of building what would become the Rideau Canal. Colonel By, under the direction of Lord Dalhousie, oversaw the development and construction of barracks to house his men in anticipation of the long-term project that would be the creation of the Canal. By 1828, the small, sleepy settlement had evolved into a more lively place known as Bytown. Farming was one of the most prosperous industries in the area, in addition to the lumber trade.

In 1855, Bytown became a city and gained a new name, Ottawa. The name change was prompted by a national debate about where the seat of government should sit. The discussion surrounding the location of the Nation's Capital included Ottawa (formerly Bytown), Montreal, and Kingston. However, in order to bring Bytown into the spotlight, it was agreed that its name needed to change so that it would no longer be tied to its logging origins. The name Ottawa was deemed appropriate and in 1857, Queen Victoria chose it as the capital of the United Province of Canada.

Ottawa was chosen as the Nation's Capital for the second time when Confederation occurred and the country became the Dominion of Canada in 1867.

Below are some important dates to note:

1826 - Bytown was formed during the construction of the Rideau Canal.
1855 - Bytown became a city and was renamed Ottawa.
1857 - Queen Victoria approved Ottawa as Canada's Capital.
1867 - Ottawa was chosen for the second time as Canada's Capital.

Photo of cab driver Mr. Reeves near the William Howe Manufacture Building on Rideau Street, ca. 1904.
City of Ottawa Archives/CA001763/James Thompson, Sr.

Ottawa is constantly evolving and
shifting; the city itself is history in motion.

FIRST-TIMERS

Visitors to Canada's Capital should begin their journey by discovering the Capital's landmarks, historical monuments, and enjoy several activities no matter the season.

Photography by Jenna Sheikh

Parliament Hill is the political and cultural centre of Canada's Capital. The Parliament Buildings (East Block, West Block, Centre Block and the Peace Tower situated on the central axis of Centre Block) sit atop a hill overlooking the Ottawa River. The Queen's Gate is the ceremonial entrance to Parliament Hill. When you walk through it you will easily spot the Centennial Flame directly ahead of you.

The **Centennial Flame** was first lit on December 31st, 1966 by former Prime Minister Lester B. Pearson, to launch Canada's 100th anniversary celebrations. Flowing water and the shields of Canadian Provinces and Territories surround the flame - these elements symbolize Canada's unity from sea to sea.

Free guided tours of Parliament Hill's Centre Block are offered daily.

Built between 1826 and 1832, the **Rideau Canal** is a UNESCO designated World Heritage Site. In the winter, the Canal freezes over and becomes the Rideau Canal Skateway - the world's largest skating rink as designated by Guinness World Records in 2005. The Canal runs a total length of 202 kilometres from Ottawa to Kingston.

Photograph provided by National Capital Commission / Commission de la capitale nationale

14

Major's Hill Park was formally established as the Capital's first park in 1875 and has been a green space since 1826. It covers about 5.06 hectares of land and offers some of the best lookout spots in Ottawa.

The National War Memorial (also known as 'The Response') was unveiled in 1939 to commemorate the contributions of Canadians in the First World War. In 1982, it was rededicated as a tribute to all Canadians that have served in times of war. Every year, on November 11th, the memorial site is where the National Remembrance Day Ceremony occurs.

Photography by Rebecca Hay

The Byward Market was established in 1826 and is one of Canada's oldest and largest marketplaces. It offers a variety of shops, restaurants, cafés, and bars. You'll find outdoor vendors selling everything from fresh produce to art. It is also a popular place to watch buskers perform in the summer.

Photography by Julia Weber

Photography by Jenna Sheikh

The National Gallery of Canada was created in 1880 and is one of Canada's oldest national cultural institutions. It displays the country's largest collection of Canadian art. One of the most notable pieces it features was sculpted by Louise Bourgeois and is called Maman. The bronze sculpture depicts a 9.27 metre tall spider carrying a sack of twenty-six white marble eggs.

Nepean Point is at the heart of Canada's Capital Region and it is approximately 1.27 hectares in size. It offers a gorgeous panoramic view of the Capital and is located behind the National Gallery of Canada. At the top of Nepean Point is a majestic statue of Samuel de Champlain.

Ottawa is home to several local and national **museums** rich with artifacts, information, and historical significance.

Photography by John Lin

Canadian Museum of History was formerly known as the Canadian Museum of Civilization. It exhibits over 20,000 years of human history. The museum is also home to the Canadian Children's Museum, which is full of educational exhibits that are fun and interactive.

Aberdeen Pavilion is one of the only nineteenth century large-scale exhibition buildings in the country still standing. It is now a national historic site that serves as a venue for various community events. The pavilion is also known colloquially as the Cattle Castle since it used to house cattle during agricultural shows.

Photography by Felixe Denson

Photography by Tony Li

The official residences are six important historic properties in Canada's Capital Region managed by the National Capital Commission / Commission de la capitale nationale (NCC/CCN). These residences are: Rideau Hall, 24 Sussex Drive, Harrington Lake, Stornoway, The Farm, and 7 Rideau Gate.

Rideau Hall is the largest official residence in the Capital Region, and it is the only one open to visitors. It has served as the official residence and workplace of every Governor General of Canada since 1867.

The house at 24 Sussex Drive was built in 1868 and it is the official residence of Canada's Prime Ministers.

Harrington Lake is located in Gatineau Park and serves as the country residence of the Prime Minister of Canada. It offers the leader of Canada a tranquil space to confer and relax in an informal setting.

Stornoway is the official residence of Canada's Leader of the Official Opposition.

The Farm has served as the official residence of the Speaker of the House of Commons since 1955.

The property at 7 Rideau Gate is the official accommodation for Heads of State and dignitaries when they visit the Capital Region.

Photograph provided by National Capital Commission / Commission de la capitale nationale

The Supreme Court of Canada is the highest court in Canada and is the country's final court of appeal.

Photography by Jenna Sheikh

The Notre-Dame Cathedral Basilica is a National Historic Site of Canada.
Visitors from around the world visit this cathedral to gaze in wonder at its
gorgeous Gothic architecture and ornamentation.

The National Capital Region features many monuments and statues that honour important figures from Canadian history.

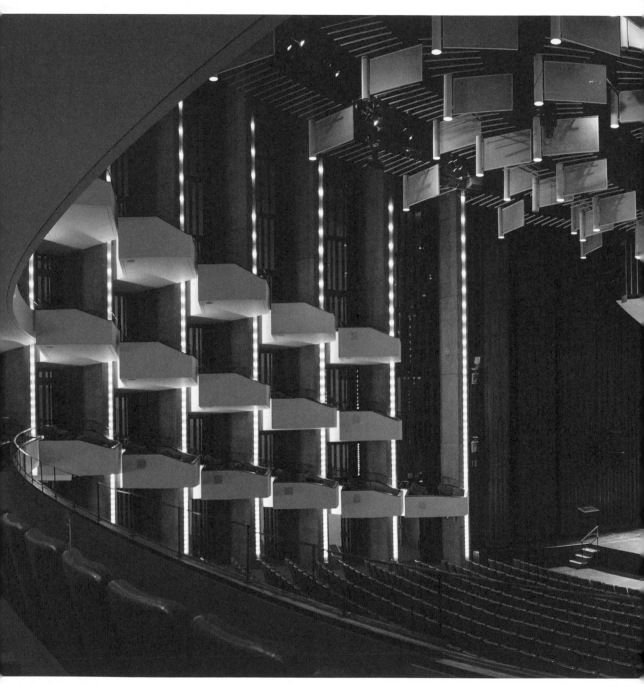

Photography by Rebecca Hay

The National Arts Centre (NAC) is one of the largest performing arts venues in the city of Ottawa that hosts a variety of productions in both of Canada's official languages. It provides a national stage for the performing arts by showcasing artistry of all forms including orchestral concerts, ballets, modern dance pieces, and theatrical shows. It also offers program development and educational activities across Canada.

Photography by Tony Li

The Corktown Footbridge was opened in 2006 and is about 70 metres in length. It spans the Rideau Canal and it is currently home to hundreds of 'love locks'. These are locks that a couple attaches to the bridge in a symbol of commitment to each other.

Photography by Tony Li

The Prince of Wales Bridge is a railway bridge that spans the Ottawa River and was opened in 1880. It is now defunct and was officially closed in 2005.

Alexandra Bridge also known as the Royal Alexandra Interprovincial Bridge spans the Ottawa River and connects the provinces of Ontario and Quebec. This structure was officially opened in 1901.

The Ottawa River passes between the provinces of Ottawa and Quebec, and it remains a waterway of historic significance in North America.

Gatineau Park is the National Capital Region's conservation park with stunning natural features, and signature plants and wildlife. It is also a great spot for hiking, camping, swimming, biking, skiing, and rock climbing. Several scenic spots in the park include the country estate that belonged to Canada's tenth Prime Minister, William Lyon Mackenzie King, King Mountain, Lusk Cave, and Pink Lake.

HISTORIC ACCOMMODATIONS

Photography by Felixe Denson

Lord Elgin Hotel was built in 1941. It was named after the eighth Earl of Elgin, James Bruce, and it has 355 guest rooms.

Sir Wilfred Laurier, the seventh Prime Minister of Canada, officially opened the Fairmont Château Laurier in 1912. It was designated a national historic site in 1980. All kinds of people have stayed at this castle-like hotel, including royalty and celebrities.

Photography by Rebecca Hay

In the heart of Downtown Ottawa is the HI-Ottawa Jail Hostel. Built in 1862, this building served as the Capital's main jail until its closure in 1972. It was eventually re-opened as an accommodative space to allow guests experience spending a night in jail.

Photograph provided by HI-Ottawa Jail Hostel

SEASONS IN THE CAPITAL

WINTER

Photography by Tony Li

There are over 150 kilometres of cross-country ski trails in the Greenbelt area encircling Ottawa. Gatineau Park, located across the Ottawa River, also has over 200 kilometres of groomed trails and heated shelters suitable for beginners and family outings.

The Gatineau Loppet is an annual event that usually occurs in February. It is Canada's largest cross-country ski event, bringing some of the very best distance racers from all around the world to the Ottawa-Gatineau area.

Photograph provided by National Capital Commission / Commission de la capitale nationale

Ice skating in the Capital during the winter season is a must-do, especially on the Rideau Canal Skateway. To further commemorate the winter season, a festival celebration called Winterlude occurs. During the festival, there are several activities inspired by Canada's history with a particular focus on traditions from the northern parts of the country. Confederation Park turns into Crystal Garden, where you find stunning ice sculptures created by professional ice carvers. There is also typically a dance and music stage at the festival along with taffy shacks and bonfires. In addition, the Jacques-Cartier Park in Gatineau also provides a Snow Kingdom full of snow slides.

Photography by Rebecca Hay

Photography by Tony Li

Photography by Tony Li

Photograph provided by OTTAWAZINE

Photography by Felixé Denson

Beavertails and maple taffies are often the go-to winter treats in the Capital.

Fun fact: Beavertails are sweet pastries that actually look like a beaver's tail.

Photography by Rebecca Hay

The Christmas Lights Across Canada program launched in 1985. From early December to early January, thousands of colourful lights illuminate the National Capital Region's winter landscape.

Photography by Rebecca Hay

Photography by Rebecca Hay

SPRING

Photography by Rebecca Hay

Photography by Daniel Effah

The Canadian Tulip Festival is one of the largest tulip festivals in the world. It attracts over 600,000 visitors every year. Each year the Netherlands sends tulips to Canada as a sign of appreciation for keeping the Dutch royal family safe during WWII. While Princess Juliana was in Ottawa, she gave birth to Princess Margriet on January 19th, 1943. In 1945, once she returned to the Netherlands, Princess Juliana sent Ottawa 100,000 tulip bulbs for providing her family with a safe haven. Thus, the Canadian Tulip Festival symbolizes a historic friendship between Canada and the Netherlands.

The Great Glebe Garage Sale is a community-run event that has been taking place in Ottawa since 1986. A variety of niche items are often for sale at this event including records, vintage clothing, and used books.

Photography by Daniel Effah

Photography by Tony Li

Photography by Daniel Effah

SUMMER

Yoga on Parliament Hill is a weekly event held in the summer that involves yoga sessions taught by yogis from all over Canada.

Photography by Daniel Effah

Biking in the Capital.

Photographs provided by Zara of XO Velo

Photograph provided by OTTAWAZINE

The Tim Hortons Ottawa Dragon Boat Festival was founded in 1993. It is a multi-day festival that involves boat racing adapted from a historical Chinese tradition. It also offers concerts, amusement park rides, sports demonstrations, and delicious culinary treats.

Changing of the Guard began as a morning routine in 1959 on Parliament Hill and has since turned into an annual summer tradition. This ceremonial march begins south of Parliament Hill at Cartier Square Drill Hall and continues up Elgin Street. The large-scale production includes Ceremonial Guardsmen that are primarily reservists in the Canadian Forces; the ceremony also includes a regimental band and pipers.

Photograph provided by Ottawa Tourism

Photography by Rebecca Hay

Thousands of people head downtown for Canada Day celebrations on Parliament Hill. Anywhere you go in the city of Ottawa, you'll see people decked out in red and white. The downtown core is always packed with people showing their Canadian pride.

Photography by Rebecca Hay

Photograph provided by OTTAWAZINE

Casino du Lac-Leamy Sound of Light is a fireworks competition that congregates pyrotechnicians from all over the world to brighten up the Ottawa-Gatineau skies.

Photograph provided by OTTAWAZINE

Photography by Tony Li

The bilingual Sound and Light Show on Parliament Hill offers a learning experience of Canada's history. This show is a visual and auditory journey that is set against the backdrop of Centre Block and Peace Tower.

Glowfair is an annual music, light, and art festival that takes place on Bank Street in Ottawa. The festival features themed blocks, stages for live concerts, and various forms of entertainment that makes it one of the city's most anticipated festivals.

Photography by John Lin

Art Battle is a live painting competition that takes place all year round in the Capital.

Photography by John Lin

The Arboretum Festival is an independent music festival that brings several Canadian musical acts together in the Capital.

Photograph provided by Arboretum Festival

Nuit Blanche is an annual, one night celebration of multidisciplinary art and local culture in the National Capital Region.

Ottawa's RBC Bluesfest Festival is amongst the largest outdoor musical festivals in the Capital. It is a multi-week showcase that features musical acts from all over the world.

Photography by John Lin

House of PainT Festival is an annual urban art festival that celebrates hip hop and brings the elements of dance, music, art, and spoken word together.

Photographs provided by House of PainT Festival

HOPE Volleyball Summerfest is an annual outdoor beach volleyball tournament that raises money for local charities in the Capital.

Photography by John Lin

Summer in the Capital is patio season; it is also known as the high point for most food festivals. Some well-known locations in Ottawa that see the most traffic during the warmer months of the year are Elgin Street, Sparks Street, Preston Street, Chinatown, Hintonburg and Lansdowne.

FALL

Photograph provided by OTTAWAZINE

Every fall season, Saunders Farm transforms from an ordinary, local farm into a site of frightening and fun Halloween antics with haunted hayrides, a Barn of Terror, and live entertainment.

Photograph provided by Saunders Farm

The Haunted Walk company offers year-round guided tours that traverse the city and serve to point out its most haunted spots. The company also offers specialized walks at historic sites in the Capital Region including Upper Canada Village and the Mackenzie King Estate.

Photograph provided by Haunted Walk

ADVENTURERS

Photograph provided by Great Canadian Bungee / Alex Potvin

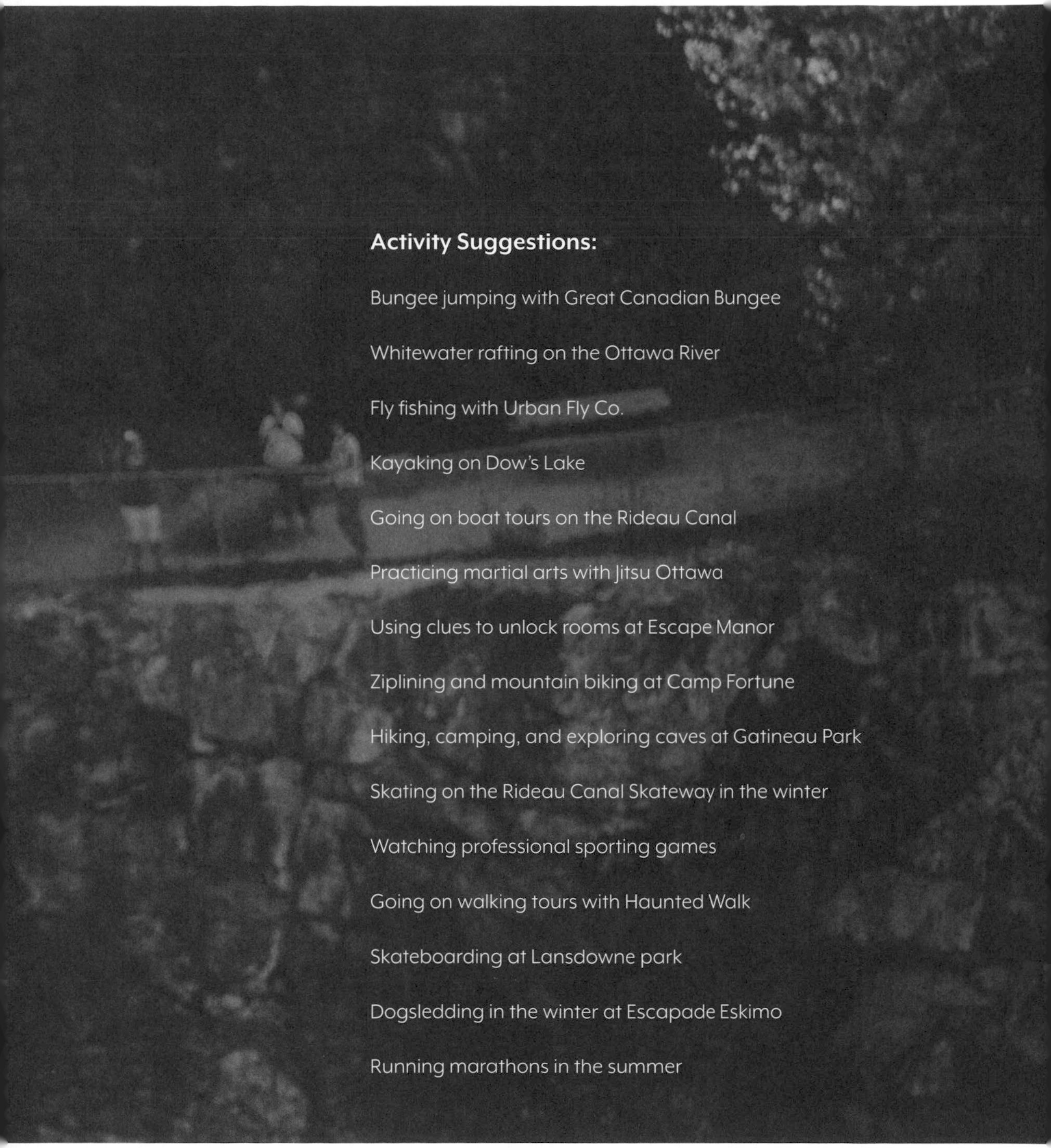

Activity Suggestions:

Bungee jumping with Great Canadian Bungee

Whitewater rafting on the Ottawa River

Fly fishing with Urban Fly Co.

Kayaking on Dow's Lake

Going on boat tours on the Rideau Canal

Practicing martial arts with Jitsu Ottawa

Using clues to unlock rooms at Escape Manor

Ziplining and mountain biking at Camp Fortune

Hiking, camping, and exploring caves at Gatineau Park

Skating on the Rideau Canal Skateway in the winter

Watching professional sporting games

Going on walking tours with Haunted Walk

Skateboarding at Lansdowne park

Dogsledding in the winter at Escapade Eskimo

Running marathons in the summer

Photograph provided by Great Canadian Bungee / Alex Potvin

Thrill seeking never satiates.

Photography by Chris Hofley

Photography by Glen Ellis

Photography by Landon Entwistle

Photographs provided by Run Ottawa

Photograph provided by National Capital Commission / Commission de la capitale nationale

NATURE LOVERS

Nature is a significant feature of Canada's National Capital Region (NCR). It is important to note the existence of the National Capital Greenbelt, a band of greenspace that forms a crescent shape within the NCR.

Spots to visit:

Hog's Back Falls	Shirleys Bay	Pink Lake
Lusk Cave	Mooney's Bay Park	Leamy Lake Park
Meech Lake	Remic Rapids Park	Jacques-Cartier Park
Dow's Lake	Morrison's Quarry	Britannia Park
Major's Hill Park	Princess Louise Falls	Rideau Falls Park
Eagle's Nest Lookout	Cardinal Creek Karst	Gatineau Park
Mer Bleue Conservation Area	Andrew Haydon Park	Breton Beach (Philippe Lake)

Photography by Rebecca Hay

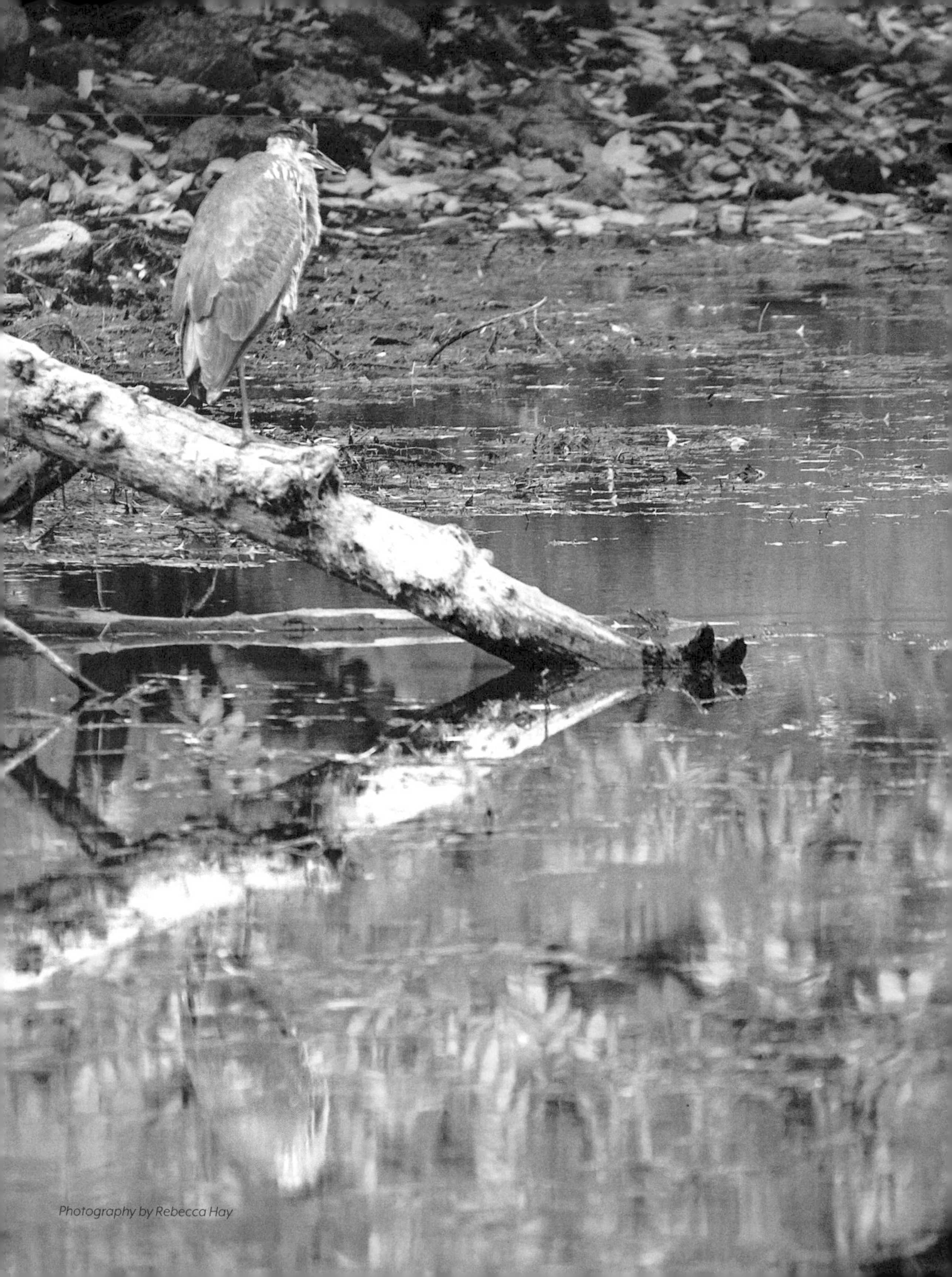

Photography by Rebecca Hay

Photography by Tony Li

Photography by Jenna Sheikh

Photography by Tony Li

Photography by Tony Li

Photography by Rebecca Hay

Photograph provided by National Capital Commission / Commission de la capitale nationale

THE CAPITAL'S CULINARY EVOLUTION

Written by Anne DesBrisay,
Author of Ottawa Cooks

So where should you eat in Ottawa? Twenty-five years ago it was a question that would have had me wringing my hands. The dining out landscape was bleak back then. So were chefs' abilities to suss out quality local product for their kitchens.

Today, the Capital's food scene presents an embarrassment of riches. Streets are lively with exciting restaurants, cocktail bars, oyster houses, food trucks, modern diners and lively bistros. Culinary festivals, food tours, community dinners, and an abundance of farmers' markets add to the vibrancy. Ottawa has emerged from the doldrums. Hallelujah. It is now a culinary destination, with a remarkably chummy chef community, a thriving bar scene and, in the past five years, a host of swish new restaurants.

The stern waiters and starched linen that once marked our high-end restaurant scene has given way to a wide pool of excellent mid-priced restaurants - places that prove daily that good food need not come with bells and whistles. In fact, we prefer it that way. Our city does come-as-ye-be, casual fine dining remarkably well. We provide high-standard hospitality courtesy of well-respected restaurateurs like Stephen Beckta (Beckta, Play and Gezellig). And for thrilling, don't-try-this-at-home dining? There is the modernist restaurant Atelier, home of two-time Canadian Culinary Champion Marc Lepine, an unassuming, unmarked restaurant that pushes every envelope. We also drink pretty well these days. Indeed, what's poured in our glasses - beer, wine and spirits - has undergone a massive change.

Ottawa has become home to a new network of world class craft brewers. The movement's been led, most prominently, by Beau's All Natural Brewery in Vankleek Hill, home of the award-winning Oktoberfest festival. In the ten years since Beau's first planted the craft beer flag in the region, dozens more breweries have set up shop. The city is now awash in good suds. And the cocktail scene - dominated not so long ago with stunning mediocrity - has very recently taken off. Passionate mixologists are shaking up well-made classics and creating cutting edge concoctions, bringing the same care and creativity to fluids as chefs bring to food.

That beer and booze expansion has been mirrored in many ways by the craft food scene, vibrant on both sides of the Ottawa River. Artisanal cheese makers, bread bakers, charcuterie masters, coffee roasters, ice cream churners, chocolatiers and fancy doughnut fryers, abound in neighbourhood shops and at the city's many farmers' markets. Ours may be the second coldest capital on Earth but it's also the only capital in the world with a working farm at its heart, a retreat of grain filled fields, barnyard animals, and experimental gardens. Ottawa has far more cultivated land, hundreds more farms and greenhouses within its municipal borders than any other Canadian city. We are a city with a backyard that is not only bountiful, but also remarkably accessible. Farmers reach our urban markets and restaurant doors with relative ease, delivering the fields and forest and gardens of the National Capital Region to urban kitchens.

As the city has matured, so too has its palate. Immigration has had much to do with this, bringing culinary traditions, ingredients and heritage dishes previously unknown. In the twenty-five years I've been a greedy observer of the dining out scene in Ottawa, intimately familiar with its strengths and weaknesses, I've witnessed, in the past five years in particular, the culinary landscape being remade. It is so much more a pleasure noshing in this city today than it has ever been. And the menu is constantly changing.

Photography by Daniel Effah

Photography by Felixe Denson

GRAPES RAISIN
PRODUIT U.S.A PRODUCE

MURE BLACKBERRIE Produce of USA

MIX AND MATCH
$2.00 /Box
3 for $5.00

RAMBOISE RASPBERRIE Produit Quebec Produce

Blueberre Bleuet Produit /Quebec Produit

FRAISE Strawberrie PRODUIT Quebec

Photograph provided by OTTAWAZINE

Photography by Felixe Denson

Photography by John Lin

Photography by Anne DesBrisay

Photograph provided by Alt Hotel

Photography by John Lin

Photograph provided by OTTAWAZINE

A 3-DAY DOWNTOWN OTTAWA ITINERARY

DAY 1: Culture & History

Begin your first day in Downtown Ottawa by exploring parts of Confederation Boulevard. The first place to visit is the Bytown Museum, followed by a guided tour of Parliament Hill. Then head to Major's Hill Park and admire every monument along the way. Upon visiting the park, stop by at Confederation Square to explore the National War Memorial. Then make your way to the National Gallery of Canada to explore great Canadian art exhibits. While at the National Gallery, visit Nepean Point for a spectacular view of the National Capital Region (NCR) and take pictures with the statue of Samuel de Champlain. In the evening, take a stroll on Sussex Drive to see the Notre-Dame Cathedral Basilica, Rideau Falls and all of the great shops and boutiques that line the street. To end the day, head over to the Rideau Canal for a sunset stroll or if you visit in winter, skate on the Canal.

DAY 2: Nature & Adventure

One of the best ways to explore the city's downtown landscape is on a bicycle due to the vast amount of bike paths present. You can do this either by biking along the Rideau Canal or by biking through available bike paths and exploring the natural elements of the city. These bike paths will lead you directly into Ottawa's green space. Another way to explore the Capital is by participating in the active walking and running culture of Ottawa, as well as going on boat tours to explore the city's landscape. To end the day, book an Escape Manor experience if you are a mystery-solving enthusiast or choose to go on a Haunted Walk tour.

DAY 3: Food & Entertainment

To conclude your last day in Ottawa, go on a food tour to explore the city's diverse food scene. Some places to visit include Byward Market, Sussex Drive, Sparks Street, and Elgin Street. Add the following to your Must-Eat list: poutine and beavertails. Then, top off your evening with some entertainment. Stop at the National Arts Centre located on Elgin Street or head into an Ottawa neighbourhood for an outdoor festival or community event.

THE PEOPLE

My journey began with the search for a home,
In search of warmth and the comfort of the cold,
Oh! Take me to the city of the people with the warm embrace,
Take me to the city of the people with glory and grace.

Thence I come to the city of glistening snow,
I hear in fall it has a fiery glow,
Yes! This is the city of the strong and the bold,
This is the city of the young and the old.

I break my gait to feel its embrace,
I bask in its air and the golden sunrays,
Today when the sun sets, I shall no longer roam,
For these are my people and I am home.

Allan André

Photography by Daniel Effah

Art came to me subconsciously. When I was younger, I remember admiring every Neoclassical painting my mum brought home. Gradually, creating art became a way for me to visualize the images I see in my imagination. The art scene in Ottawa is very receptive and everyone is like family as opposed to a bigger city, where it might be harder to be heard; it's easier to make bigger waves in a small pond like Ottawa.

So far, I've been able to connect with a lot of people in the city through art and I'm most noted for being a past winner of Art Battle, an art teacher at several Paint Nite events, my showcase at the Ottawa Art Gallery and Fritzi Gallery, live paintings at several museums in the Capital Region, Nuit Blanche, and I am one of the creators of the famous Sandra Bland mural in Ottawa.

Presently, I'm working on creating a hub that will serve as an open studio that facilitates creative discovery. It's important that the community has a shared fertile ground that grants them the right to grow, and offers a creative sandbox that gives them the license to have fun and play without being graded, as well as helps spark the courage in them to make mistakes. I believe perfection can be paralyzing and with this hub, I hope to inspire people to take a leap into the unknown and discover something new inside themselves.

Josiah Marquis

Photography by Daniel Effah

I found the transition from high school to my undergraduate studies to be very demanding. I seriously considered dropping out of university the first month of my biology program because I felt out of place and purposeless. I was able to stick it out though largely because of the support I receive from my peers.

As I continued with my education, I began to cultivate interests in human physiology and psychology in the context of health and wellness. This interest connects to my passion for skateboarding, which has been my main creative outlet for over a decade. It has taught me many great lessons that have translated into other areas of my life. It is also one of the things that helps to ground me and keep me tethered to the here and now. Skateboarders, in my experience, tend to exemplify positive character traits like resilience, persistence, and creativity. There is also an amazing amount of diversity amongst skateboarders. With local skateboarding companies leading initiatives through charity and mentorship programs, I am excited to continue to watch the skateboarding community thrive in Ottawa as the years go by.

I am also happy to announce that with intense determination I was able to improve my academic standing from being on academic probation to making the Dean's Honour List.

Saveeta Sharma

Photograph provided by Saveeta Sharma

As I dance so does my soul. I founded Upasana (The Spirit of Dance) in 1995. It is dedicated to the preservation and promotion of Indian culture through the ongoing development of Kathak, Odissi, and my own innovative style of contemporary dance. I consider myself a teacher first and foremost, and a dancer and choreographer second.

I began to dance at the age of four. Pandit Birju Maharaj, a renowned dancer and guru mentored me in Kathak. Then, I went on to receive a Baccalaureate in Dance in 1987 from the University of New Delhi, where I also acquired a master's degree in dance. After graduating from school, I moved to Ottawa in 1990. I eventually went on to study ballet upon my arrival in Canada.

It feels great to see students enjoy themselves and learn at Upasana. My dance school provides a structured curriculum of dance to its students. Over the years I have seen the appreciation for art and the performing arts rise in Ottawa and it is very encouraging. It is also humbling to be supported by the City of Ottawa, Ontario Arts Council, the Ontario Trillium Foundation, Canada Council for the Arts and Canadian Heritage. Ultimately, dance is a form of self expression that enables rich personal growth.

Stephen Graham

Narrative and photographs provided by Stephen's daughter, Emilie Graham as told by her grandmother, Mimi Graham

When Stephen was ten years old, he spent most of his time watching the speed skaters practice on a 400 metre oval at Balena Park in Ottawa. He knew then that speed skating was the sport for him and so he saved every penny to buy himself a pair of skates. Every Saturday his Dutch Opa gave him a dime and he saved those dimes until he had $22 - just enough to buy a used pair.

In 1971 no matter the temperature, he could be found at the rink every evening. Before he knew it, he was a member of the provincial team, the Canada Games team, and had participated in international competitions. He was also a part of the Ottawa Pacers Speed Skating Club and continued in this club as a coach.

Stephen subsequently received a degree in electrical engineering from the University of Ottawa and he is now the father of three girls. Not only was he a skilled skater, he inspired people as the little boy saving dimes for a dream.

Jasmine Mah and Catherine Zadeh

Photography by Daniel Effah

Between the two of us, we have been doing pole fitness for approximately ten years. It was something we decided to try and never looked back. We both lead busy and successful lives but coming back to pole fitness is always our escape.

The pole fitness community in Ottawa is inclusive, and accepting. Contrary to its general associations with stripping, pole fitness has been a source of empowerment for us due to the physical and psychological benefits of the exercise. It has also been very refreshing to notice a steady growth in people from all walks of life visiting the Ottawa Pole Fitness Studio.

Our hope is to challenge stereotypes, raise awareness of the physiological benefits of pole fitness, and encourage people to begin to recognize pole fitness as a sporting activity in its own right that incorporates dance, gymnastics, circus arts, and a variety of other forms of exercise. Pole fitness builds confidence, strength, self-esteem and has truly contributed to an overall improvement in our quality of life.

Debbie Owusu

Photograpy by Daniel Effah, Debbie Owusu, Elfreda Tetteh & Mariline Buvat

As a first generation Ghanian-Canadian, I know that Ghana is just as much my home as Canada. I am currently pursuing an undergraduate degree in Women's Studies at Carleton University and with my degree, I have been able to not only explore the worlds of marginalized women, but also expand my horizons as a Black female activist.

Topics like feminism, racism, and sexuality play a vital role in every aspect of my life's journey. I am also currently a program coordinator at the Womyn's Centre at Carleton University. Through this position I have been able to create several projects with talented people in the campus community and the Ottawa community. One project I helped with is called Black Women Intersections.

This project began in early 2015 when Black History Month was just around the corner and I noticed that public discourse focused on a plethora of accomplished Black men and only a handful of Black women. Even if these women were recognized, they were often Americans. We used this project to raise awareness on the distorted view of the type of women celebrated in the media by photographing Black women of varying identities in an unapologetic manner.

We exhibited the photo series on campus and constructive conversations began. Our project gained traction not just for its aesthetic qualities but for its message.

Julie Beun

Photograph provided by Julie Beun

I left Ottawa in 1988, vowing to shake its dust off my Doc Martens for good. Now, I can't imagine a better place to live, work and raise a family. In the eighties, Ottawa was a microcosm of the world - more of a tiny pinhead, really. But in the indie/alt music community, we had what my friend, the late lamented music impresario Nadine Gelineau, called 'our tribe' - a motley bunch of music lovers, nascent bands, suburban rebels and loudmouth punks like VICE owner Shane Smith that clung together to make life bearable at CKCU and noisy hole-in-the-wall bars such as Nadine's Banana Obscuri, or Le Zinc in Vieux Hull. They were the best of times, full stop.

The Swans and Henry Rollins at One Step Beyond. The Smiths at the Congress Centre and Billy Bragg at Porter Hall. Nina Hagen wailing away at Nepean Point and manic road trips to see the Cure. Hanging out at the Nervous Onion under Barrymore's with people who would later become something really big, like Shane and Nadine, and people who found their perfect groove and stayed in it.

Even so, when I graduated from Carleton University, my head was filled with possibilities that Ottawa did not offer. So I left. I was twenty-one, had $400 in cash and a return ticket when I moved by myself to Australia, to work as a journalist. At that time, Australian journalism was gritty, dynamic and competitive, based on the Fleet Street model. By God, I loved it. Battling for scoops with the big boys, breaking stories, landing the front page; it was a defining time in my career.

Being a journo Down Under was what we called a 'holding a blow torch to the underbelly', but it was also more fun than a bag of drunk monkeys. So why did I leave my beach house to return to Ottawa? I get that a lot. Look around. It didn't happen overnight, but Ottawa is interesting. Ottawa is dynamic. Ottawa has possibility. I never thought I'd say it, but Ottawa is pretty damn cool these days. Sure, there are the great little restos, neat buildings and vibrant history that sets one city apart from others. But Ottawa has heart because of its people...almost twenty-five per cent of whom come from another country altogether. We're a city that loves to throw galas and give generously to charity. We are diverse in our interests, from hockey and baseball to our passion for art and theatre. Having battled with the talent drain for years to places like Toronto, Montreal and Vancouver, Ottawa is now attracting astonishingly creative people, who add immeasurably to our cosmopolitan, multi-coloured little metropolis. In the end, I'm not sorry I left Ottawa. But I'm sure as hell glad that I came back.

Sheridan Grout

Photography by Barrie Martelle of EDM Photos

I've been a DJ in Ottawa for about six years now and I originally started while in university, but then I got noticed by some big name bars and it all took off from there. The DJ community can be competitive, especially when it comes to being a Trance DJ. I've played in Montreal but I mostly play here in Ottawa, which is nice because it's a good feeling to look out at the crowd when I'm up on stage and see people I recognize, who consistently come out to support my music.

Some of the best experiences I've had in Ottawa have come on stage, playing alongside some of the biggest DJs in the world at Barrymore's, and off the stage where I frequently enjoy the great patios the Byward Market has to offer with friends. In my opinion, as a city, Ottawa offers you a lot from beavertails, the Rideau Canal, Lansdowne and of course the Byward Market. Musically there is a lot that happens in the summer in terms of festivals - Escapade and Bluesfest to name a few. I've lived in Ottawa all my life and even with my music taking me out of the city a lot, Ottawa is still one of my favourite places to perform. This city is truly a great place to be and to live.

Side note, I'm also an accountant - but I guess everyone has to have balance right?

Alanna Sterling

Photography by Jenna Sheikh

Ottawa is my home; It is the city where I was born and raised, the city that I've explored inside and out, and the city that has seen my music grow into what it is today. At three years of age, I started taking piano lessons. At ten, I picked up the guitar. And at twelve, well, that's when I first started combining my poetry with my guitar to write songs. Since then, I've written over a hundred songs. When I finally turned nineteen, I sought out all the open mics in Ottawa. Any stage I could play at was a stage I would be at. Through the open mic scene, I honed my craft, I overcame any tiny shred of stage-fright I had and my passion was fuelled by the audience's applause. I was also inspired by other musicians and made a lot of connections that have helped guide me to where I am now.

I practice like it's my religion. There's not a day that goes by where I don't sing; it's how I express myself, how I ground myself, and it gives me a purpose in this crazy world. I feel like music is the one thing that can be shared with everyone. There is not a single person on this planet that hasn't been moved by music in some way; and I think that's what makes it so beautiful - it's universality.

When I am not singing or performing, I am pursuing an undergraduate degree in Biomedical Sciences with a specialization in Neuroscience at the University of Ottawa. It has been a challenge balancing music and education, but it has been fun. I released my debut album in February 2015. Each album case is handcrafted using recycled cardboard, velcro and glue, and I also design each CD face individually. This way, I am supporting sustainability and a concrete piece of my imagination becomes a part of each album. In November 2015, I started a band so I could reach new levels that were nearly impossible to reach as a solo act. We're called Alanna Sterling & The Silvers; I play guitar and sing, but also have the opportunity to play saxophone and trumpet with the band.

There is so much talent in Ottawa but it is also a rough place to turn music into a career. Not enough people come out to live performances. My advice to everyone is to go out of your way to support a local artist. Simply showing up is all it takes to give an artist the courage to keep following their dreams, and with your support we can make the music scene flourish.

Jessica Vermette and Jenna Hutcheson

Photograph provided by Jessica Vermette and Jenna Hutcheson

There is no emotion quite like the satisfaction you feel when you make something with your own two hands. As co-founders of the Ottawa Makers Market, we aim to use our seasonal markets to help showcase artisans, and local crafts makers to the Ottawa community. Every vendor that contributes to the market is very invested in their product. There are no hobby crafters or part-time Etsy artists, the market is full of people that have created new and exciting businesses that are aiming to bring the idea of making things back to the forefront of society. Our markets serve as a great reminder that despite the fact that somethings are indeed easier to buy online nothing ever truly compares to placing that last flower into a bouquet for a wedding party or hammering that last nail into place for a rocking chair.

In addition to running the Ottawa Makers Market, we also operate a floral design company called L'Orangerie.

Chantal Sarkisan

Photography by Emma Haidar

I moved from Toronto to Ottawa about fifteen years ago. I studied biochemistry in French at the University of Ottawa, where I eventually met someone, got married and established my family here. I never thought I would stay in Ottawa this long, but my husband was not keen on moving.

At the time, I liked that Ottawa was a very safe and clean city, so I didn't fight to leave but I must admit it was an adjustment to settle down here. I felt that there wasn't enough for me to do. It was very quiet and seemed to lack the busy cultural atmosphere that I was used to having been raised in Downtown Toronto. That's when I decided to take matters into my own hands and become a local tourist. I started leaving the house and I started blogging to really highlight gems in the city.

Fast forward to now, the new Ottawa. Between all the local festivals, revived spaces, upgraded fashion landscape, indie fairs, and local fundraisers, the Ottawa we see today is completely unrecognizable. While I was bored, I took matters into my own hands and decided to make this place work for me. I got out of my comfort zone. I was curious. I met people and kept an open mind throughout my explorations. I encourage everyone in the city to do the same thing. You'll be surprised at how much there is to discover.

I eventually founded Mode XLusive, a blog where I try to capture and showcase the unique fashion and beauty elements of Ottawa.

Katie Hession

Photography by Syed Zeehad

After years of living away from Ottawa, it was nice to return to all the things that made it my home growing up. I was born and raised in the west end and during my twenties, I moved away to study and travel the world. I always knew that I would one day return to Ottawa because I have deep roots in this city, and it was where I knew I wanted to raise a family. I moved back a few years ago, married with two beautiful kids. Upon my return, I picked up my camera again and began to use it to rediscover my hometown. What resulted is my photoblog, YOW City Style, a project showcasing Ottawa street fashion and lifestyle. This has provided several opportunities for me like being invited to Tel Aviv Fashion Week, having my own column in Ottawa At Home magazine and collaborating with some very interesting individuals.

YOW City Style uncovers all the hidden gems in the pretty little, big city I call home. It has a Human of New York feel to it with a focus on profiling fashionable Ottawans and discovering interesting shops, restaurants and events that the locals love. In an increasingly homogenized world, our local businesses, restaurants and hundreds of amazing makers and artisans, are what make our city unique.

I love the variety of activities that are open to us living in Ottawa, from great family friendly activities to fun nights out with my friends, and dates with my husband. We live close to Lansdowne so we love to take the kids over to the farmers' market or the 613flea on weekends. I also love how it's very easy to escape the city for outdoor activities like hiking in Gatineau Park or having a beach day at Meech Lake. The energy of our city is at its peak during the summer festival season and you can usually find me checking out my favourite musicians, hunting down my favourite food trucks, and taking street snaps of all the great fashion I see go by.

Judy Hum-Delaney

Photograph provided by Judy Hum-Delaney

I founded Ottawa Foodie Girlz in 2014 to merge my interest in event planning with my interests in fundraising and food. Currently, we are made up of seven members and our goal is to experience the best of Ottawa dining while making connections with local restaurants and businesses. Ultimately, we hope to use these connections to host food related events benefiting local charities.

Our city is vibrant with an incomparable food scene complete with award-winning chefs and vast cuisine options. If I were to choose some of our favourite spots to hangout, it would be Fiazza Pizza, Absinthe, Holland Cake & Shake, Moon Room, Two Six Ate, and Elgin Street Diner to name a few. We also love to support our friends in the Bytown Chefs Collective.

To date, we have hosted six events raising more than $11,000 for various organizations including: Harmony House, The Ottawa Mission, and the University of Ottawa Heart Institute. We really believe that food brings people together.

Jose Martinez

Photography by Rebecca Hay

In my experience, it is easier for other people to influence you and direct your life if you do not truly know who you are. I am a very outspoken gay man who is active in the LGBTQA community in Ottawa. My involvement began at the age of seventeen when I was looking to volunteer at the AIDS Committee of Ottawa to fulfill the volunteer hours I needed to enroll in the social work program at Algonquin College. Prior to this time, I was unaware of the LGBTQA programs and services offered in the Capital but the AIDS Committee soon served as an excellent platform for me. It was there that I learned of one of their subdivisions called "Gayzone," where they offer rapid, anonymous STI/HIV testing for homosexuals. Not only that, they also offer a safe space for gay people still in the closet.

One of the benefits of the city of Ottawa is that it is small and so it offers a slower pace for people to take their time and become accustomed to its nooks and crannies without feeling rushed. My advice to every homosexual still in the closet who feels alone is that they take advantage of Ottawa's pace and and not feel afraid or intimidated to get out there and take advantage of the services and programs available. Some of these services include: The Canadian Centre for Gender and Sexual Diversity, Ottawa Senior Pride Network, and Kind.

I also have a lot of appreciation for everyone that is involved with the LGBTQA programs and services in Ottawa because all of their time and energy pays off.

Melanie Bejzyk

Photography by Ima Ortega

One of my favourite places in Ottawa is "The Village" on Bank Street. I love it for all of its rainbow crosswalks on the street, rainbow flags flying high, and the rainbow business signs gracing cozy coffee shops, bars, and restaurants. It's especially beautiful in the summer what with the colourful festivals that frequent the area.

After several years of having been held in front of City Hall in Ottawa, the annual Ottawa Capital Pride community festival was brought back to Bank Street in 2015 with the generous support of the City of Ottawa. In my opinion, the Ottawa Capital Pride festival is as much a protest as it is a celebration. It's an acknowledgement of the improvements made toward more equality and human rights but it also serves to help people recognize that stigma and discrimination still exist in Canada and around the world.

In 2015, I volunteered to help make human rights an integral part of the festival. So, with the help of a few photographers, neighbours and friends, we held free workshops for kids and spoke to many people about human rights. We also opened a booth at the festival where we encouraged people to express their thoughts on human rights and their vision for them. The amount of support and participation was overwhelming. I remember a young person sharing a message in remembrance of a gay friend she had lost to suicide and what she wrote in her message was that "love is love." I believe Ottawa not only recognizes this message, but is an embodiment of it.

The photos we collected at the booth paint a picture of the mosaic that our local community looks to embrace. Our vibrant community in the city displays the spirit of the LGBTQA community with all of its triumphs and challenges, boldness and colour.

In 2017, Canada celebrates 150 years as a nation. I believe that the Ottawa Capital Pride festival will provide every citizen of the city a platform to express our pride.

Noel Paine

Photograph provided by Noel Paine

Ottawa is a running town. All you have to do is stand outside on the sidewalk when the sun is shining in front of Parliament Hill and watch as hordes of runners pass by. The city hosts Canada's largest marathon and a great percentage of the people who compete are local runners. In fact, the whole area just naturally lends itself to runners with so many multi-use trails, the Rideau Canal to run alongside or on in the winter, Gatineau Park's paved and hiking trails, along with the Rideau Trail right in our city's backyard.

I've been running since I was twelve years old - I'm forty now - and I have run marathons and 100-mile ultramarathons in Boston, the Grand Canyon, Ireland, and Italy. I can tell you that Ottawa holds its own with the best of them as a great place to lace up, stretch, and compete. I am proud and privileged to be an ambassador for the Ottawa Marathon that takes place in May, and the Army Run, which happens here in September. So, if you're a runner, come and challenge yourself in both. You won't be disappointed.

A bit about myself - I grew up on the salty shores of Nova Scotia and moved here in 2009 as an Air Force officer (Captain). I was released from the Canadian Forces two years later and now suit up as a civilian for the federal government, like many others in Canada's Capital. My wife, Stephanie, our new daughter, and I are now snugly nestled just across the Ottawa River in Gatineau, which has its own unique charms for living and running.

I take a break from manning a cubicle during the day by running to and from work and often also run also at lunch, throughout the region. To mark my fortieth birthday, I ran from Kingston to Ottawa on the Rideau Trail; covering 258 kilometres in just over two days. My other passion is for writing; profiling runners with stories to tell, for a weekly blog for the Canadian Running magazine. The main attractions that draw runners to the city are the elite level and exceptionally well organized Ottawa Marathon and Army Run. But there are also many smaller, unique events that happen here, like a winter marathon, snowshoe races, and a race just outside of Ottawa where all of of the runners involved wear kilts while racing.

If you're staying in Downtown Ottawa as a visitor, just head out the door and run up and around Parliament Hill, along the Rideau Canal or pop over the number of bridges to Quebec and suddenly you've pounded the pavement in two provinces over the course of one run. There are great green spaces and parks everywhere too. So, I invite you to come to our magnificent Ottawa, I am always looking to meet new runners.

Jabez Willy

Photographs provided by Jabez Willy

Football came to me at a time when I would get into all kinds of trouble because I needed an outlet to expel my energy. I grew up in Montreal and only moved to Ottawa about a year ago to complete high school. Right away, I signed up to play as a line backer for the Glebe Gryphons, my high school's football team.

I presently play for the Ontario Varsity Football League with the Cumberland Panthers as a running back, and I have been able to attract the attention of multiple scouts from several universities in Ontario including the University of Ottawa, and Carleton University. Nonetheless, the biggest highlight for me has been playing at the TD Place Stadium at Lansdowne park with my Gryphon's team mates.

What I think people need to remember about life is that you know you are good at something when it keeps coming back into your life.

Corey Sheikh and Michael Alemao

Photographs provided by Ottawa Lifestyle Centre

Four years ago, we never dreamed that the Ottawa Lifestyle Centre would grow into the community fitness hub that it has become. At our centre, it's not about the destination, but the journey. We embody this mentality by helping people achieve their full potential and encourage them to concentrate on the process instead of the outcome. Our initial intention was to start a boxing studio but when Mike and I partnered up, the vision transformed into a holistic fitness hub for lasting change in our clients.

Our holistic approach sets us apart. We are not a gym; we are a lifestyle centre. Mike and I have worked hard to build a team of like-minded individuals to create a place for the mind and body to fulfill themselves. As long time residents in the Capital Region, we wanted to bring something unique to the Ottawa fitness landscape, and so far, Mike and I have accomplished just that at the Ottawa Lifestyle Centre.

153

Rob Spittall

Photography by Syed Zeehad

As a kid, I developed a strong passion for comics and my dream was to open a comic book shop. After working in retail for over a decade, I partnered with my boss at the time, Steven Ethier, to open our very first comic book shop in 1999. Our goal was to create a safe space that was accepting of everyone. If we can accept comics with stories of green people shooting lasers from their eyes, why not accept real people?

We also try to squash stereotypes about comic fans, especially the notion that women are not fans of comics. In fact, we have more female employees than male ones in the store, and we also host several functions for women with a 'No Boys Allowed' sign on the door. The Capital Region as a whole has a welcoming attitude, and that is the same attitude we try to capture at our store, whether it be hosting a ladies night function, a mental health awareness event, photoshoots or a movie shoot, we welcome everyone.

Vaughn MacDonald, Alexandra Ekstrom and Steven Yong

Photography by Rebecca Hay

Black Squirrel had its start as Bibliocracy in 2011, a little shop on Somerset West that was stocked with Vaughn and Steve's personal book collections. After quickly outgrowing the space and a desire to have a more distinct Ottawa feel, we renamed it Black Squirrel Books and settled at Bank and Sunnyside so that we could also incorporate a café.

We owe the success of our business to the community of Ottawa, because people here are very supportive of local businesses. The welcome we've received from the community as an alternative to chain bookstores and coffee shops has been great.

We only brew and sell locally roasted coffee and we get our baked goods from several bakeries around Ottawa. In addition, we have great connections with local writers and musicians, so we regularly host poetry readings, book launches and workshops. We're truly proud to have Ottawa as Black Squirrel's home.

Dr. Alfonso Abizaid

Photography by Rebecca Hay

I am a professor at Carleton University in the Department of Neuroscience, where I supervise a research lab that is interested in how the brain regulates food intake, body weight, and energy balance in response to a number of challenges.

I've lived in Ottawa for almost a decade and it has been wonderful to experience all of its thriving hospitals and post-secondary institutions. In order to continue to promote the advancement of science and research within the community, I was part of the group of people that created the Ottawa chapter of the Society for Neuroscience, one of the largest neuroscience organizations in the world.

The Ottawa chapter aims to educate people about the brain, promote mental health awareness, and help bridge the knowledge gap that exists between the scientific community and the public. One great advantage of living in the Capital is that it is an important place for research, because we are close to policy makers, so we have the opportunity to advice these policy makers with sound research.

When I am not at my research lab or promoting an event with the Society for Neuroscience, I am volunteering as a coach for my children's hockey and soccer teams.

Lindsay Banks

Deciding to become a nurse was something I knew I wanted to pursue, mainly because I've always loved helping people. The most rewarding moments of the job happen when you meet people for the first time in critical states and they get nursed back to good health after coming to the hospital.

Even though being a nurse has not been easy because nurses are continuously challenged to be the best they can be for their patients, there is nothing that will compare to forming long-lasting relationships with patients and developing deep bonds with them. I love hearing stories from my patients who are always willing to talk about their lives as if we weren't meeting for circumstantial reasons at the hospital.

Perhaps it is because most of my patients are from Ottawa or perhaps it is because they are just genuinely kind people, I have learned that if I accept patients as they are they will accept me too.

Ottawa Popscope

Ottawa Popscope began as an urban movement in 2014 to connect the Ottawa community with the night sky. We started with a set of two telescopes, now we offer multiple telescopes that help us engage with an even bigger crowd at our pop-up events.

We generally identify as students and professionals by day and astronomy enthusiasts by night. We are not only astronomy enthusiasts but community enthusiasts too. We want to give back to people that also enjoy conversing about space and astronomy by engaging in strategic partnerships that offer the safe utilization of urban public spaces in the city. Not every urban resident has a telescope and not every student or civilian has an equal chance at becoming an astronaut or astrophysicist. So, we believe in sharing the knowledge of what we know with others while also having fun.

Come join us with #ottawapopscope in watching the night sky.

Samantha Banning

Photography by Rebecca Hay

When we moved into our current home five years ago, I was very anxious about how we were going to fit into our new community. There were no other children in our building and my eldest son, Alawi, being autistic, wasn't always aware of how his noise level affected people around him. I immediately introduced myself to our neighbour across the hall and explained about Alawi to her and she responded with a smile. She told me that the only sounds she hears coming from my apartment were of laughter and that it was wonderful to have a happy family living next door. It has taken some time but Alawi now runs around our neighbourhood having fun just like all the other kids his age.

The community centres in our neighbourhood are open to having respite workers attend after school programs, and with this one-on-one support, Alawi has been able to attend art classes and Lego Robotics courses. These classes coupled with the incredible support of his instructors have encouraged Alawi's interest in computer programming.

Some of my favourite things to do with the boys include, sledding at Lansdowne, swimming at the wading pool behind our place, going to Dow's Lake to paddle boat, getting beavertails by the Rideau Canal, and dipping caramel apples at the Whole Foods Market on Bank Street.

Having a child with special needs teaches you to appreciate the beauty and wonder of everyday life. As a parent, you have to learn to slow down and once you do, you realize how much love and joy there is in the simple things. Just laying under a tree, staring up through the branches at the sky, I realize that allowing my child to set the pace brought me a whole new perspective on life.

Annie Wheeler

Photographs provided by Annie Wheeler

When Eleanor was six months old, a large mass was discovered in her abdomen. We spent almost seven months at both the Children's Hospital of Eastern Ontario (CHEO) in Ottawa and The Hospital for Sick Children (SickKids) in Toronto to nurse her back to health with the support of very incredible staff at both hospitals. The doctors told us that the mass was attached to her liver and it was causing all sorts of problems with her other organs. After scans, blood work, ultrasounds and many tests, Eleanor was given a differential diagnosis of hepatoblastoma. We created a Facebook group called "Eleanor's Epic Quest" that helped keep our family and friends updated on Eleanor's situation, and soon we had over 1,300 people supporting her. Our daughter is now known as "Epic E".

Eventually, the doctors informed us that it wasn't cancer we were dealing with, but a rare and benign tumour called mesenchymal hamartoma. The diagnosis took a long time to be confirmed but after the tumour was removed, we really learned about the power that love and support can bring. Even if there is not enough data on mesenchymal hamartoma for us to be certain of what the future holds for Epic E, she has taught us that life is precious and that tomorrow is never guaranteed. As a family, we aren't sure what our future will look like but we are making sure to live life to its fullest.

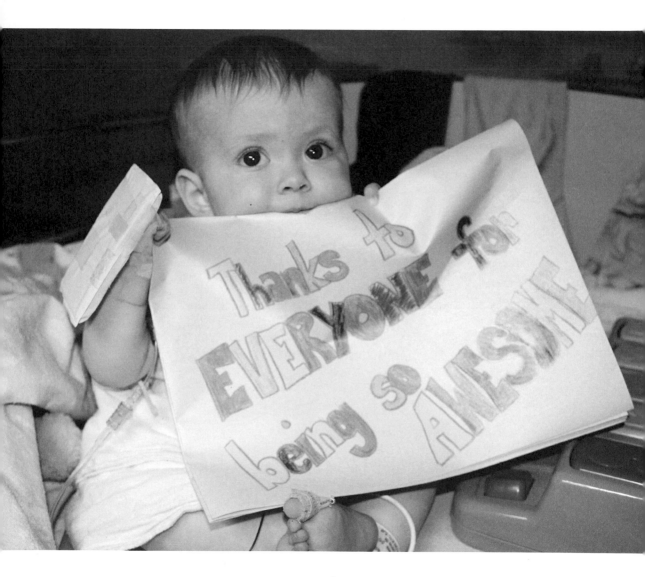

Raymond Lin, Leon Li and Yuanchen Zhu

Photograph provided by OTTAWAZINE

We founded OTTAWAZINE for Chinese people, specifically those that have recently moved to the city of Ottawa, to fit into the community seamlessly. It also serves to promote local Chinese businesses and organizations.

Presently, OTTAWAZINE is one of the most popular Chinese media platforms in the Capital with WeChat being one of our most successful channels to reach our audience. Ottawa has been a great start for us as it has offered us an excellent business environment to connect with the right audience. However, our goal is to become a global media group that provides incredible content to our audience with a mission to bridge the communication gap between Canadian culture and Chinese people.

Kimani Peter

Photography by Daniel Effah

Growing up in an economically depressed neighbourhood in North York, Toronto inspired me to create better opportunities for myself and for my peers. So, I moved to Ottawa on a mission to make use of its encouraging climate for entrepreneurs to build a company of my own. This led to the creation of my brand, ONYX, which is an umbrella concept that helps creative minds interact and work together.

This brand also includes several offshoots, one of which is called LOUD; it takes a smart approach to outdated business models used by record labels by linking technology and music with artists and other music enthusiasts. The goal is to eliminate the need for major record labels, and empower emerging artists to create without fear of exploitation from these labels.

It's the twenty-first century, so making the music experience smarter is essential. My overall goal is to encourage people in and outside the city of Ottawa to tap into their experiences to create a better future for themselves and to encourage people to create art without regret.

King B. Hector Jr.

Photography by Lunatiqsoul

As CEO and Creative Director of the Ottawa based fashion brand, We Are Kings Inc., I work to promote cultural diversity and inclusiveness in the city. We Are Kings Inc. is a menswear brand I founded because of my love for blazers and suits as well as my passion for empowerment. Through this brand, I am able to make use of ethical production and fair trade practices while prioritizing the rights of workers and safe workplace conditions. My designs and fabric choices are both inspired by my Nigerian roots. My vision is to make African print an accessible and everyday clothing choice so that anyone could walk on streets anywhere in the world and see people wearing apparel made with African fabric both corporately and casually.

Since launching my fashion brand, the people of Ottawa have been extremely supportive. Everyone here is receptive to new entrepreneurs and it is for this reason that my brand continues to thrive. Fashion industry leaders like Angie Sakla Seymour, Director of Angie's AMTI, gave me my first ever runway experience. Then, Julie Beun, Daytime Ottawa host at Rogers TV gave me my first television interview, and Sarah A. Onyango, radio host & producer of CHUO 89.1 FM gave me my first radio interview. These are only some of the people who have helped my business grow.

I have presented at fashion shows in other cities like Montreal and Toronto but I truly believe that the fashion industry in Ottawa has a lot of potential. I have noticed a resurrection of the fashion industry in Ottawa because people are recognizing the impact of fashion and are doing something about it.

As a creative mind when I am not promoting my brand on runways, I usually unwind at the National Art Gallery. This is one of my favourite spots in Ottawa. Ottawa is my home away from home, I will always remember where it all began.

Jaime Koebel

Photography by Felixe Denson

I was born in Lac La Biche, Alberta and I am of Otipemsiwak/Nehiyaw descent. I moved to Ottawa in the early 2000s and I have never left. I founded Indigenous Walks in 2013 after my time as an Educator for Sakahan at the National Gallery of Canada. There are several Indigenous exhibitions at the Gallery and I truly enjoy educating people about Indigenous issues. So, the idea behind Indigenous Walks was to continue to educate people, and to take them on a journey through Downtown Ottawa to inform them about local landmarks and stories from an Indigenous perspective.

A typical walk begins at the Canadian Tribute to Human Rights monument on Elgin Street, and ends at the National Gallery of Canada. Other spots you might visit on a tour include the Canada Council of the Arts, National Aboriginal Veterans monument, Confederation Park, National Arts Centre, and Major's Hill Park.

Ottawa truly offers a lot to do and see, but most importantly the aboriginal community is vibrant here and there is a diversity of First Nations, Métis and Inuit from across Canada in the Capital.

Lynn Jatania

The best blogs tell a story through a series of scenes, perhaps a few hundred words that each come together over time to paint a picture of a complete life.

In Ottawa, there's a diverse, vibrant, and passionate blogging community where it seems everyone knows everyone - and much of that is thanks to Blog Out Loud. I founded this event in 2009, and it's an annual evening of live readings of the top blog posts from the past year, selected by a panel. It is also a space that allows every author to interact with their audience face-to-face.

I believe that the short essay format of a blog post can easily capture emotion and create a personal connection between an author and a reader. There's no doubt that these little gems of writing have invoked everything from delight to anger to grief to side-splitting mirth in the audiences at every Blog Out Loud event. There's plenty of time to socialize at Blog Out Loud too. There's always a moment to say hello to old friends and meet other bloggers who already feel like old friends. There's also the chance to be a fan and meet your own fans, and to discover cool new blogs to add to your reader's list. Past events have featured such well-known and enduring Ottawa ambassadors as Andrea Tomkins of a 'Peek Inside the Fishbowl', Dani Donders of 'Postcards from the Mothership', Amanda Jetté Knox of 'The Maven of Mayhem', and Ross Brown of 'The Brown Knowser', but many smaller bloggers have been featured too. These people are writers with clear voices and important stories that might have otherwise been overlooked if not for Blog Out Loud.

Blog out Loud events have been held in the past in several Ottawa locales such as Irene's Pub, The Prescott, and the Raw Sugar Café (now sadly defunct). In recent years, the event has moved under the banner of the Ottawa International Writer's Festival, which has put our local authors on a level with writers from around the world, and helped confirm the idea that a blog post really can be a thing of beauty.

Everyone is welcome, so come out to Blog Out Loud and listen, laugh, and - if you have your own blog and you're feeling bold - maybe you will dare to take the mic yourself.

Tammy Giuliani

Alessandro and I met when I was travelling through Italy in 1985 - he was cruising the streets of Rome on his Ducati, and I was strolling around visiting the sites. We went out one night for pizza and gelato and three days later, he asked me to marry him. After a decade together in Rome, we moved to Ottawa to start our family.

Learning about gelato has always been one of our passions. With a goal to bring authentic gelato from centuries-old recipes to Ottawa, I returned to Italy a few years ago to train with some of the country's finest gelato masters. We're nearing our fifth anniversary at Stella Luna and our greatest achievement so far has been receiving the bronze medal for the Americas in the Gelato World Tour that took place in Chicago in May 2016. Our bronze medal allows us to advance to the finals of this competition where we will represent Canada in Italy in 2017. We set out a few years ago to create a space where neighbours could gather for a handcrafted, old-world style gelato; we never expected to be recognized as one of the top three gelato shops in the Americas!

Years ago, a client mentioned how she wished she could bring Stella Luna to her wedding and as a result, the idea of our vintage gelato push-cart was born. Our vintage carts are on the road all summer with freshly prepared, handcrafted gelato. We attend weddings, corporate picnics and events, area festivals, farmers' markets, and private gatherings. No matter what celebration you're having, gelato is a treat that almost everyone enjoys.

Ottawa has been extremely generous to Stella Luna. The neighbourhood welcomed us with open arms and even after five years, people still travel out of their way for gelato at our shop. The fact that people are willing to wait in line for over half an hour to get gelato on a hot summer's night from our café is a testament to the community's support of Stella Luna. We're off to Italy in 2017 to represent Canada in the Gelato World Cup finals and are exploring options for expansion. We've started offering our gelato to some of the higher-end restaurants in the city and of course we'll continue to roam around with our vintage gelato carts.

We'll just keep dreaming of the stars and the moon (Stella Luna!).

Sam Turgeon-Brabazon

Photograph provided by Sam Turgeon-Brabazon

Following an environmental science class on sustainable agriculture in high school, I wanted to help make fresh, organic greens more accessible to people as well as find a way to perform hassle-free urban farming. So, I learned to sprout seeds and designed a prototype called Sam's Sprouts that I have now cultivated into a business. Organic micro-gardening is a fun process from rinsing your seeds, setting them on a windowsill to harvesting - seeing the fruits of your labour flourish couldn't be more exciting.

I am a full time student at Carleton University in the Public Affairs and Policy Management program. Through my specialization in Human Rights, I am able to draw a connection between my business and ecological rights. I think my love for gardens started when I was a kid, and I try to include my childhood gardening experience in my product. Inclusivity, ecology, economic viability, and versatility are key aspects of my business; my motto is to always keep it "Organic, Simple, and Fun." We also translate this motto in our hand packaged kits that focus on reducing waste and reusing materials. Whether it is the glass growing jar, the plant-based, compostable seed bag or the multi-use filter, we try to encourage you to remain sustainable and grow a healthy food that you can add to your diet.

Eric Koch and Will Porter

Photography by Jenna Sheikh

We are best friends who live in Orléans, but we are better known by our company, a takeout restaurant called LunchBox Ottawa. We have a lot of past experience in the Ottawa food industry and we felt that our love for cooking could be channeled into our own project.

LunchBox Ottawa provides people an alternative from packing lunches and going on expensive lunch outings at work, school, or anywhere else by offering an eclectic food menu to choose from. Anyone can request one of our packaged lunches for a future date or for immediate delivery as we try to be as available as we can to people in the city leading busy lives. We also try to provide a warm and welcoming restaurant that is accepting of everybody.

Ottawa is a city with many boroughs and pockets rich with vibrancy, diversity and acceptance, and we are so humbled to be a part of this city.

ourse Syllabus
Lunchbox Upgra
$3.00
Snacks
eef, crispy onions,
orseradish sauce
$10.00
balsamic mayo
$9.30
·Apple
and green leaf lettuce
old cheddar
spinach, raspberries,
peanuts, banana
$8.85
t chicken, berry
ens, $9.75
st pork,
onions,
breast,
rry-herb ma
ickén, roast
pper,
e, tomato,
n relish, $8
Available
amy Potato Salad
antain Chips
ovie-Style Popcorn
Salad
$2.50
Slaw
$2.50
& Apples
$2.50
& Veggies
ie Doughs
Fave
Show

Grace Lam

Photography by Jenna Sheikh

I came to Ottawa from Hong Kong forty years ago so that I could attend Algonquin College. I ended up getting married after college and became a housewife. However, I eventually decided to go into esthetics. I've noticed that esthetics in Ottawa is thriving and I think it is because people are afraid of aging, more now than ever before.

I've had clients for about thirty years because they notice the good work I do for their skins. Being an esthetician is partly like being a psychologist. My clients tell me about themselves and their problems, and because of this openness, I am able to cultivate good relationships with them. In essence, being an esthetician has a hidden personal aspect to it.

Looking back to when I first came to Ottawa, the city has changed quite a bit, for one, there are more people now. Ottawans are very nice too, but the weather? Lousy. In spring, it feels like winter, so who knows what's going on up there in the sky!

Alyssa Spaxman

People often ask me how I got started with Strut Jewelry, and it's hard to answer that question because I've made things with my hands for as long as I can remember. I've always felt the need to create in my bones, and still do. I was the kid who couldn't just sit and watch TV. Instead, I would spread out beads on a tray, and attempt to wire-wrap them into necklaces for hours. As I grew up, I continued to try to make new things but the one thing that I always returned to was jewelry.

I began my company slowly in 2009 with a few pieces listed on an Etsy shop and a table at the local farmers' market at Lansdowne Park. I remember those initial weeks, making a few sales here and there, and being completely blown away that people actually wanted to buy what I made. It was incredible! As response grew, so did my business, and the Ottawa community has played a big part in my journey as a creative business owner. There is so much support and love for local businesses here, and I'm so grateful to be a part of this vibrant and beautiful city!

My jewelry is inspired by travel, nature, and architecture. I love the moment when someone tries on a piece and it fits them perfectly and they just light right up.

Jamie Pistilli

Photograph provided by Jamie Pistilli

A lot of people don't know that the Ottawa River hosts at least eighty-six different species of fish that range in size from two inches long to four feet or more. This river is also a great spot for musky fly fishing and it has attracted several fishing enthusiasts from all around the world.

I started Urban Fly Co. about a year ago with one of my good buddies, David O'Sullivan and it has been a great source of education for us and our customers. We share in the work because David makes all of the flies, which are typically about twelve to fourteen inches long, and I take people to do the actual fishing. Our tours typically include a trip from Downtown Ottawa past Arnprior or as far as our customers intend to go.

The coolest fact though is that about 250,000 Americans travel up through North America to go musky fishing and Ottawans don't even know that we have one of the greatest musky fly fishing spots on the continent.

Esha Abrol

Photograph provided by Esha Abrol

I started my first company, a consulting business, while I was still an undergraduate at the University of Ottawa and since then my passion has been entrepreneurship. I have both founded and helped found successful tech companies in Ottawa and I have been lucky enough to watch the tech industry grow tremendously over the years. Being involved in the business industry has given me the opportunity to share my story in several publications and has allowed me to meet some fantastic startups from around the world, including Silicon Valley. I also organize business events regularly and I often cross over into the real estate industry to help tech companies seek out investment opportunities in that market. My aim is to help Canadian tech companies break into the global marketplace.

When I am not involved in the business side of things, I am teaching the Argentinian tango at Carleton University or doing background work as an actress for television films. As a born and raised Ottawan, I truly believe that my city has a lot to offer to just about anyone and that in itself is the true beauty of the Capital.

Rachel Décoste

Photography by Tony Li

As a child of immigrants from the third world, I've come to quickly understand the realities of giving back and increasing discourse on topics of concern for minorities. I am specifically passionate about increasing the recognition of Black women in print and online media. I grew up in Orléans, Ontario and in the eighties and nineties, there wasn't much diversity in my neighbourhood. In fact, at that time, that lack of racial diversity encompassed most of Canada. I believe that it was only after the post-Pierre Trudeau immigration wave that Canada accepted a large amount of non-white immigrants. My passion for advocacy and philanthropy stems from my childhood and from my parents' mantra to help thy neighbour. They served as foster parents for over twenty years and this selflessness instilled in me compassion and a sense of duty towards others.

I also believe in equality for women. I'm for equality across the board, so I make sure that women's voices, especially those of Black women, are heard just as much as everybody else's. Back in the day, it was hard to find anybody of colour present their opinions in national op-ed sections. So, one of my childhood goals was to call attention to equal representation in all spheres of Canadian life.

When I am not working as a software engineer during the day, I am writing articles for the Huffington Post on issues that are often ignored by other media outlets. I use the power of my pen and keyboard to allow my voice to shine.

Amanda Parriag

Photography by Tony Li

Media Action Média is a national nonprofit organization that was established in the 1990's as Media Watch. Since then we have changed our name so that we are no longer watching, we are taking action. We run programs that amplify women's voices across the country and increase the positive representation of women in the media. We have two active programs, the National Informed Opinions Program and the Ottawa-focused Ask Women Anything program.

The National Informed Opinions Program works to train and support women by making their ideas more accessible and fostering their leadership capacity. On the other hand, the Ask Women Anything program is focused on spotlighting women from the Ottawa community who are experts in different areas, without a media filter, in an intimate environment so that they can chat with the community at large. We aim to engage the Ottawa community and highlight the incredible wealth of expert women we know but don't get to hear enough from.

Our goals are to bridge the gender gap in public commentary and enhance the quality of public discourse by expanding the diversity of perspectives that inform Canada's policies and priorities. We deliver engaging keynote presentations, dynamic and practical workshops, ongoing editing support, and strategic advice. In Ottawa as in the rest of the nation, we aim to make women part of the public discourse.

Nina Kressler

Photograph provided by Ottawa Convention Centre Corporation

I grew up in Halifax, Nova Scotia, where I graduated with a Bachelor of Arts Degree from Mount Saint Vincent University. Back in the eighties - in the early days after my graduation - jobs were very difficult to find so I happily accepted an entry-level position at a hotel. Even though I had no hospitality experience and thought my career path might lead another direction, I was certainly excited by the prospect of a challenge. It didn't take me too long to fall in love with the hospitality industry so I remained in the field and continued to advance my career from various administrative roles to eventually taking on the role of Vice President, Sales, and Marketing at Trade Centre Limited. In 2011, I took a position in Toronto; about two years and a half later another opportunity opened up in Ottawa and the rest is history.

I am currently the President and CEO of the Shaw Centre, an Agency of the province of Ontario that reports to the Ministry of Tourism, Culture and Sport. Our mandate is to drive economic impact for the city of Ottawa and the province of Ontario, and my job is to oversee a team that aims to bring international conventions here, as well as national, regional, and local consumer and trade shows.

Shaw Centre's focus on customer service sets us apart as a convention space. We currently rank 4.7 out of 5 in overall customer satisfaction and that is mainly because of our attention to detail and customer enhancement programs we've introduced to our convention centre. For example, we offer complimentary pashmina scarves to people attending meetings to address the challenge of achieving a perfect room temperature for all. This is a particular challenge when 3,000 people are meeting in a 58,000 square foot room. We also offer complimentary reading glasses to those who may have forgotten their glasses, cell phone/tablet charging stations, and a seating space created with Adirondack chairs produced by a local carpentry company that help the centre's visitors take in a view of Downtown Ottawa via our panoramic glass façade. Additionally, we give back to the community every year by working with programs like Mealshare, and we donate a broad range of items no longer in use from conventions, meetings, and events that take place at the centre. Our commitment to customer service has led us to achieving the coveted Service Excellence Award in 2016 from the Ontario Business Achievement Awards.

Ottawa has truly become my second home. It is a city that is meant for everyone and with the current expansion of the city to include Light Rail Transit (LRT) stations, and the LeBreton Flats development project, this city will become even more vibrant than it is now. The fact that our current mayor, Jim Watson, is also one of the most engaging mayors I have ever encountered also sets our city apart.

Although I spend a lot of time at my job, which I love because it is all about hospitality, I make sure to unwind whenever possible. There is nothing like walking down the Rideau Canal in the summer and seeing the beautiful boats that come from all over Ontario and parts of the United States. Even walking down the Rideau Canal in the wintertime is equally fun since you can watch people skate to work with their morning coffee in hand.

My overall goal as President and CEO of Shaw Centre is to continue to work with our strategic partners at Ottawa Tourism and our hotel community to positon Ottawa as a key player in the international and national convention arena. We are well poised to attract new businesses and visitors to our beautiful city. If I can do that, and also help lead Shaw Centre to being awarded the first place prize for best convention centre in the world by the International Association of Congress Centres in 2018 - we are currently tied for second place - I know I accomplished all I set out to do when I moved here years ago with my family.

Michael Crockatt

Photography by Noorulabdeen Ahmad

I began my career in the aviation industry, first with the Winnipeg Airports Authority, and then with the Ottawa International Airport Authority. In 2015, I joined Vancouver-based InterVISTAS Consulting, solidifying key learnings about inbound tourism and the visitor economy. When the opportunity arose to become President & CEO of Ottawa Tourism, I jumped at the chance to join this fantastic team.

I truly believe that Ottawa is a great place to celebrate every momentous occasion in Canada's history, a great four-season city, a city with amazing festivals, and a city with great cultural depth. Almost every day, I find something new in this region. For example, one of my favourite spots is the unique Diefenbunker, Canada's Cold War Museum.

One major thing that sets Ottawa apart is the spirit of collaboration and partnership that intersects across industries and stakeholders here. It also helps that Mayor Jim Watson understands first-hand the value of tourism and its economic impact, ensuring that tourism initiatives are integrated into the fabric of the municipality. These collaborations and positive partnerships definitely do not happen in every city.

Ottawa mixes an intriguing cocktail: Canada's national museums (including one of the world's best art galleries), a vast amount of greenspace, extensive urban and rural recreational paths, and a diversity of cultures representing the people who make their homes here.

Our job at Ottawa Tourism is to attract people to Ottawa by offering a complete capital experience, telling the story of Canada, and getting people talking. When visitors share their stories and enthusiasm about Ottawa with their own networks, they inspire others to travel here.

The year 2017 is a special year for Canada, and especially for Ottawa, as the country celebrates its 150th birthday. The events that will be hosted all year round in this city are going to be absolutely spectacular, and they will certainly be a part of how we continue to tell the story of Ottawa into the future.

I invite you to join Ottawa Tourism in the conversation and share your Ottawa gems. Be sure to connect with us on Twitter (@ottawa_tourism), Facebook (visitottawa), and Instagram (@ottawatourism) to add your voice and ideas with the hashtag #MyOttawa.

Mark O'Neill

Photography by Noorulabdeen Ahmad

When I moved here from Toronto in 1970 as a seven-year old with my parents and six siblings, I remember reading a sign from the car that read the population size of Ottawa was about 197,000 people. My mother cried for a week. We had just left a city with over a million people that was on the brink of becoming cosmopolitan.

By contrast, our opinion about Ottawa was that it was a cold capital where there was nothing to do. Fortunately, our minds soon changed when we began to form our roots here, and Ottawa has grown so much since then. Some of the things I enjoy doing in the Capital include walking around Westboro in the summer, exploring art galleries, going to Gatineau Park, attending the RBC Bluesfest music festival and checking out the Tanger outlet mall for some good shopping deals.

I have seen the city grow from being a very big town with a large rural area to a small city rich with life. About a million people now live here and I have witnessed the maturation of the Capital Region. Even though the Capital Region continues to evolve over time, certain elements that make it distinctive still exist like its inclusive atmosphere and its sense of community.

One of my favourite memories about Ottawa was Project 4000, which happened back in 1979. I was only sixteen years old at the time and I remember hearing Mayor Marion Dewar's call to action speech that urged us to help the Vietnamese, Cambodian, and Lao refugees who had fled the Vietnam War. At the time, Ottawa had, according to my recollections, minimal cultural and racial diversity, so Project 4000 was a big deal for the city. It was a municipal project that involved everyone working together to resettle the refugees. I believe that project was a defining moment for Ottawa because the whole city was willing to put in a lot of work to enrich our communities by welcoming new people into our neighbourhoods and our lives.

As CEO & President of the Crown Corporation that operates Canada's national museums of human and military history, the Canadian Museum of History and the Canadian War Museum, which includes the Canadian Children's Museum, the Virtual Museum of New France, and the Virtual Museum of Canada, I want to be able to present the Canadian story from various perspectives. History is constantly unfolding; it never stops and we are all a part of it. For this reason, our museums continue to adapt the way that they convey the history of Canada. In 2017, we will unveil the Canadian History Hall. This Hall is roughly about 40,000 square feet and was architecturally designed by renowned architect, Douglas Cardinal. It will tell the story of Canada like it has never been told before; by allowing multiple perspectives and multiple voices to shine through we have created a more dynamic and inclusive exhibition. Ambitious in scope, the Hall will use multiple perspectives to explore some of the darker chapters in Canadian history, such as residential schools, as well as important advancements like the Truth and Reconciliation Commission, the emergence of social justice advocacy, such as the struggle for LGBTQA rights, and Canada's presence on the international stage.

My focus with exhibitions like this one is to encapsulate all of the changes that our country has undergone and explain to Canadians and international visitors alike how we have learnt to carry on, despite our mistakes, to build a functional and inclusive society.

Mayor Jim Watson

Photography by Rebecca Hay

I moved to Ottawa in 1980 to pursue a university degree in journalism and communications, and since then, I haven't left. In fact, my family eventually moved here to join me. My drive to serve Ottawa pushed me to get involved with politics, and soon enough I became the youngest mayor in the city's history.

Ottawa continues to shape itself and evolve into a place that offers something for everyone. Some of my favourite things about Canada's Capital include our respect and preservation of heritage, the Parliamentary precinct and the sub-communities and sectors that exist within the Capital. This city is unparalleled and it should serve as every Canadian's second home. Visitors also get the best of both worlds with Quebec on the border and the Francophone community as our neighbours.

Personally, some of my favourite spots in the city include Watson's Mill in Manotick, the Diefenbunker museum in Carp and the East Block on Parliament Hill. If I were to describe Ottawa in three words, I'd say Ottawa is fun, historic and innovative.

We are incredibly proud to be a part of the wonderful police force in Ottawa. For us, it's about helping the community everyday and seeing a positive change come from our hard work. Being a police officer makes us feel proud and in all honesty, we are so lucky to be living in Canada.

Between 2012 and 2013, we went to South Sudan on a United Nations (UN) mission to help train their emerging police force. As part of that international mission, we worked with officers from all around the world including Japan, Brazil, Australia, and Bangladesh. This mission brought a wealth of cultural understanding to our force back home. We have an amazing team of officers with us here in Ottawa, and we don't say this lightly given that we've worked with officers from all over the world.

Our mission is first and foremost to help and protect, but we're also part of the community. We are deeply involved as parents, volunteers, and sports coaches. Ottawa is an amazing city, and we feel grateful to serve here in our Nation's Capital. The Rideau Canal is undoubtedly a favourite place for us to spend time, whether it's running down the boardwalk during the summer or skating with family in the winter. We are also partial to the Army Run, which takes place each September. But truth be told, it's the people, the food, the festivals, and the community as a whole that make Ottawa such an amazing place to live.

Kevin Williams and Rob Hagarty

Photography by Jenna Sheikh

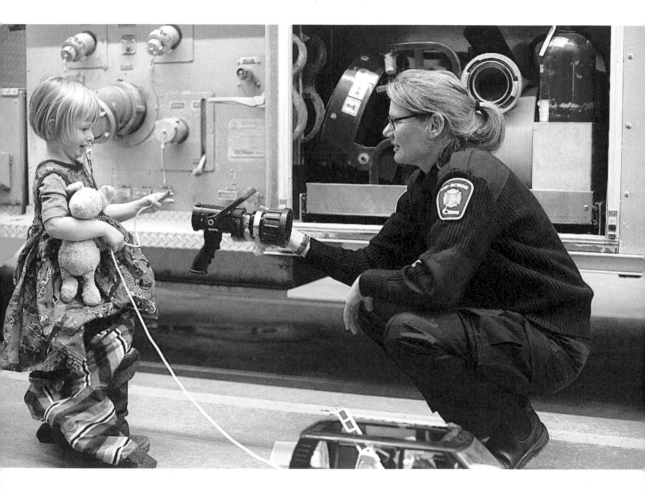

Louise Hine-Schmidt

Photograph provided by Louise Hine-Schmidt

I have been a firefighter since April 1999, and I am currently an acting lieutenant stationed in the west end of Ottawa. My career involves responding to many different types of fire related, rescue and medical assistance calls. I work all over the city and every day is so different, which is what I love about my job. Some emergency calls can have a lasting impact, but with good coping tools and a great family support system in place, I am very fortunate to still enjoy my work. Most of the time people are happy when we show up to help and that's a pretty nice feeling.

Once, on Canada Day we rescued people stuck in a hotel elevator, and from start to finish they were still having the time of their lives dressed up in red, white and maple leaves, despite being sweaty and confined to a small space for over an hour. Many people in Ottawa have that positive attitude.

I personally love Ottawa because it is a little/big city and it offers so much. I love that my city supports an active lifestyle which is how I prefer to live. No matter what time of the year you visit, you will always have something to do here.

Elias (Eli) Merhej

I've lived in Ottawa for twenty-eight years now, and I love it here. It's a very clean and friendly city. I was born in Lebanon and I came here with my family in December of 1988. There was a civil war back home, and I first moved to Syria but I didn't feel very welcomed there. In Canada, you can have freedom, real freedom; you're free to do what you want. All I knew about Canada before coming here was that it is a cold country with lots of snow. But, I also heard lots of very good things about Canada so, I applied to move here when I was about thirty years old. It took three years but now Canada is my home.

I worked three jobs when I first came to Ottawa, but I've had my own business here for almost six years now. I've been a tailor since 1970 - all my working life. I didn't speak a word of English when I first came here to Ottawa but I learned the language from other people.

Canada Day is my favourite day of the year in Ottawa. I love to celebrate it with my family and friends. We take a lunch basket and go downtown at eleven o'clock in the morning with all the other people and stay until eleven at night, after the fireworks are finished. Very simply put, for me, Ottawa means freedom.

Hassan Hassan

Photography by Noorulabdeen Ahmad

As a refugee and genocide victim from Darfur, Sudan, I knew the moment I migrated to Canada with my family that I had to do something for my Sudanese brothers and sisters back home. I grew up in displacement camps and never truly had a sense of security all of my childhood. There are several people who are still suffering back home and I knew I needed to help.

I was about nineteen years old when we moved to Winnipeg, Manitoba and it was there I completed high school and began an undergraduate degree in Leadership and International Organizational Management from the University of Manitoba. I knew that real change for my country needed to begin with people like me - people who had the opportunity to leave the country for a better future. So, I became a human rights activist. However, I knew that my best shot at accomplishing this role would require moving to Ottawa, so I moved. I've never regretted my decision.

I moved here in 2015 and it wasn't long afterwards that I formed the non-governmental organization called Sudan Allied Youth. The goal of this organization is to empower Sudanese youth around the world to utilize digital media to raise awareness for our country. Today, there are chapters of my organization in four continents but the majority of the supporters who helped grow this organization are all here in Ottawa. This city has definitely changed my life as it is helping me realize my dream for my country, and for my Sudanese brothers and sisters waiting for change to happen.

Marianne Klein

Photography by Rebecca Hay

As a Brazilian who lived in the city of Ottawa for a year to complete my PhD studies, I think Ottawa is one of the best places I have ever lived. Before moving to Canada's Capital, I knew more about the cities of Toronto, Montreal, and Vancouver combined than the city of Ottawa.

Now that I am back in Brazil, I remember Ottawa for its beautiful tulips, the Rideau Canal, its cold weather, its architecture, and people's kindness. I will never forget the kindness of the stranger that helped me navigate my way back to my PhD lab after I had gotten lost on the Carleton University campus.

To me, Ottawa represents accomplishment because it was there that I accomplished one of my dreams - the completion of my doctorate degree. It was also in that city that I met some of my best friends today. Living in Ottawa was a better experience than I could have ever imagined.

Claire Leunissen

Photography by Rebecca Hay

I recently gave a speech about my Franco-Ontarian identity at the University of Ottawa's FEDTalks event. I used to get defensive about my French accent, about remembering the right vocabulary, and about using the correct verb tense. I didn't fit in London, Ontario - my hometown - and still don't feel like I fit in university amongst French speakers from Quebec. Honestly, 'Soyons Fiers, Soyons Franco-Fiers' has become a personal mantra that I repeat to myself everyday to keep my chin up and my head high.

Writing my FEDTalks speech taught me how to embrace my identity; I felt completely vulnerable up on that stage. I even got sentimental when I concluded my speech by saying that I only learned to value my French culture once I realized I couldn't be myself without it. Being a Franco-Ontarian will always be a part of my thoughts and my values.

Judy Palkovich

I am originally from Pittsburgh, Pennsylvania. I met my husband, Tom, from Ottawa nineteen years ago online. Until then, my only experience with Canada was Toronto - a much larger city. During our four-year long distance relationship before we married, I had the pleasure of spending a lot of time in Ottawa visiting with his friends and family, shopping, dining, and touring the many sites, green spaces, museums, galleries, as well as experiencing the culture and festivities the city has to offer. It has become my adopted second home.

I love Ottawa. It holds such charm and beauty. The people are so warm and welcoming. I love its diversity, its historical flair and focus on green living. Year-round, there is always something to see and do: from Winterlude to Canada Day, Remembrance Day to the Canadian Tulip Festival - we visit often and never run out of ideas for new adventures.

Ottawa will always hold a special place in my heart for all of the memories that reside there; I got engaged to my husband at the Greek Souvlaki House in 1999. My father-in-law still resides there, and our nine-year old son has come to love Ottawa over the years as much as we do. His first skating experience was on the Rideau Canal at Winterlude when he was two years old.

Ioana Cialacu

You hear it all the time -
"Ottawa's so boring."
"There's nothing going on."
"At least it's close to Montreal."

I used to think that way too. I hated my first two times living in Ottawa - it was cold, miserable, and there was nothing to do. I was cranky and wrapped up in my university bubble. And then, when I visited the third time, I realized that Ottawa is humming with energy and there is always something going on as long as you know where to look. Check out a Japanese cult film at the Mayfair theatre, and fill up on Stella Luna's gelato on the way home. Bust out your best mask for a Lucha Libre night in Vanier. Hit up a vernissage at the Orange Art Gallery (bonus-free snacks!), or for something heartier, grab a sandwich from Dirienzos and go kayaking down the Rideau Canal.

Ottawa's charm is in its diversity - it is like a jack-of-all-trades, dotted with museums and underground experimental shows, poutine trucks and artisanal doughnuts. Actually let's talk about the food some more. It might not be Montreal but, just like your favourite grandma, Ottawa will feed you until you can no longer eat. From shawarma places that are open until three o'clock in the morning to El Camino tacos, Ethiopian food offered on Rideau street, pho, oat ice cream, and the ubiquitous beavertails, O-town's culinary scene has got something for everyone.

I've been lucky enough to live and travel to lots of places, meet amazing people, and see amazing things. Even so, crossing the bridge to Hull, and looking back at Parliament Hill, Notre-Dame Cathedral Basilica, and the National Art Gallery, I can't help but feel how lucky I am to live in Ottawa. Because I've fallen so hard for it, I give long, off-the-beaten-path, overly enthusiastic tours to my friends. If you don't have friends in town, hit up couchsurfing, or meetup groups - find someone who's passionate about this city, and can show you its hidden gems. You'll never be bored here again.

Mary Cook

Ottawa is truly a part of me. I've grown up here and I've worked here. Every time I leave the city and return, I know that I've come back home. I've lived all over Ontario, and it was in Sarnia, Ontario that I discovered what I love to do, and that is storytelling. When Alan Maitland hired in 1956, I was the tenth female broadcaster in Canada and eventually brought my craft and experience back to Ottawa in 1959 where I worked for CBC for forty-eight years.

I honed the art of using a tape recorder to discover ordinary people with extraordinary stories. I also soon realized that it was a very different and powerful experience to interview someone on his or her own turf rather than in the radio station's studio. Meeting people in their element, seeing their eyes light up, and touching upon their emotions taught me that everyone has a story to tell.

Ottawa is a very rich community filled with many human-interest stories. I have earned the right to call myself a storyteller and I bring stories to life through broadcasting and through storytelling with the Young At Heart website. The people and places in Ottawa that I am familiar with inspire the short stories I write for my column, and I am proud to say that all eleven of my books have become Canadian best-sellers. I have deep-seated ties with this beautiful city, from the National War Memorial, to Andrew Haydon Park, to the Somerset Street Bridge - it's all a part of me.

Ottawa has changed; it has grown bigger and has burst into a bustling metropolis. Despite all this growth though, it will always have that small town atmosphere that I know to be my home.

Christina MacLean

I was born and raised in Ottawa and although I love to travel, Ottawa has everything I need to enjoy life. When I was five, we moved to Bells Corners, which was "way out there" according to my grandmother. As a youngster, I learned to love the National Capital Commission (NCC) bike paths that meander along the Ottawa River and other areas. We'd peddle from the eastern to the western end of the bike path (close to Andrew Haydon Park, which is a fabulous place to picnic by the way). Then we'd bike towards the city, stopping in at my grandparents' home in Britannia for a quick snack, and then continue all the way to Parliament Hill before turning back. Sometimes we brought breadcrumbs to feed the ducks.

Now I live in the east end of the city, just a stone's throw from the eastern half of the bike path. In the winter, we also cross-country ski or snowshoe along the snow-covered pathways. On summer evenings, my husband and I love to head out for after supper bike rides. Sometimes we head east and ride all the way to Orléans. For a change of pace, we head west towards the Prime Minister's residence or the Byward Market for some refreshments.

In recent years, we started to take the bike path to join in on the amazing Canada Day celebrations in the streets surrounding Parliament Hill. The NCC maintains the pathways along the Rideau Canal too, and I used to live very close to the Canal in my twenties. In the summer, I'd strap on my roller skates and head to work along the Canal and in winter, I sometimes skated to work on the ice. How can you beat that type of experience? It combined fun, fitness, and convenience!

I love that Ottawa is a big city but it's also a small community in many ways, especially in my business, the defence and security sector. You get to know everybody quickly, and that's great. I've met a lot of people who came to Ottawa for a work term and instead of leaving when their term is up, they decide to stay!

I'm also a principal at Beacon Publishing. I've been immersed in the publishing industry since I was twelve years old, helping my dad in his print shop on weekends and I loved it. I worked for other magazines before I started FrontLine magazine in 2004 to deal with and discuss issues of national defence and public safety. Being a female in a very masculine community hasn't hindered me in any way; I've always been accepted and treated with respect.

If you're coming to Ottawa, check out the Mer Bleue Conservation Area in the Greenbelt. There's a boardwalk that meanders through the marshes. You'll probably see a beaver, maybe a muskrat too, and if you're lucky, a deer or a moose.

Kerry MacLean

While my mother insists that I'm a Maritimer since I was born in Saint John, New Brunswick, I have in fact spent all of my conscious life in Ottawa - with a couple of brief exceptions. I grew up in the Vanier-Cyrville area. During the sixties, there was still plenty of green space and community spirit that led to parades, carnivals and lots of active sports for young people in that area. From Eastview, we moved to Cummings Avenue just on the Gloucester side of the boundary. This was the best place to grow up - a field, a forest, and a stream all ran along the National Capital Commission (NCC) parkway - and it was a world of adventure to explore via my 3-Speed Mustang. Summers were spent outside from dawn to dusk while winters were for playing road hockey and building snow forts until we froze.

Busing to school in Beacon Hill North and the brand new Henry Munro school was the most inconvenient part of my life then, but it did open my eyes to a whole new part of the city, the 'East End'. It was there that I also made a multitude of lifelong friends. Then we moved to a place called Orléans, filled with plenty of potential friends that shared my love for sports and outdoor adventures.

My only time away from Ottawa was spent at McMaster University in Hamilton and one year in Kingston, which taught me what an amazing town Ottawa really is, and how I had taken it for granted. Ottawa is precious to me because of the variety of things you can do all across the city. Culture and cuisine are very abundant here, and the museums, theatres and festivals keep our entertainment options wide open all season long. Who doesn't love Winterlude and the Rideau Canal?

I also think that being on the border with Quebec defines Ottawa in many ways. There is a cultural nuance in Gatineau that lets you know you are in a different city and province. The people are amazing and the geophysical difference of the Gatineau hills makes you feel like you are on a vacation or a sightseeing trip every time you cross the Ottawa River. I also enjoy the variety of the Ottawa Valley, from the nearby farmlands and cottage country to the downtown nightlife.

As a grown up, I have spent my adult life in the pursuit of play and sports. As a physical education teacher for twenty-nine years, I helped grow and develop the high school sports scene. On top of that, as a hobby, I founded the Maverick Volleyball Club in 1985. The club is now one of the largest in Canada with twenty-five teams and close to 1,500 participants in our learn-to-play programs across Ottawa. The people of Ottawa have been big supporters throughout our growth and we are now striving to create a permanent home for the Club.

Elizabeth Radtke

Photograph provided by Elizabeth Radtke

Ever since moving to Ottawa in 2011, I became very involved in campus and community life at the University of Ottawa (uOttawa), where I recently won the university's Leadership and Inspiration Scholarship. I am originally from Waterloo, Ontario, where my parents still live, but I spent my childhood growing up in both Waterloo and Thessaloniki, Greece.

I am a strong believer in getting involved within your community and making lasting personal connections. As a student, I was on the executive boards for several student associations, Editor-In-Chief for the online magazine, Her Campus uOttawa, studied in China, and worked in South Africa for the United Nations High Commissioner for Refugees (UNHCR). I have served on several international delegations in the U.S., Israel, Palestine, and Turkey. It continues to be humbling and rewarding to represent Canada on a global level. These experiences allowed me to attend World Bank and International Monetary Fund (IMF) Annual Spring Meetings in Washington D.C. in April 2015. From January to August 2016, I worked for the Member of Parliament for the Riding of Waterloo, and the Minister of Small Business and Tourism on Parliament Hill. It was very gratifying to be able to help make decisions for my country and forge lasting connections with several MP's, Ministers and dignitaries in Canada.

When I am not working or traveling, I love exploring Ottawa; it truly is a big city with a small town feel. By adventuring out of downtown, you will find that Hintonburg and the Glebe are beautiful neighbourhoods. Biking is also a good activity to do in the city as there are so many bike paths. Nonetheless, the Parliament Buildings are my favourite spots in the city, as you get to see Canada's democracy in action. While I have now moved to Paris, France to pursue a master's degree, Ottawa will always be my home away from home.

Nabil Imani

Who am I? To some I am a guy with a 9-to-5 job, and to others I am the nerd who loves superhero movies that hugs his PlayStation 4 to sleep. But most of Ottawa would recognize me as the founder of the Young & Awesome social group, which I have been running for the past five years. It started with three strangers meeting for coffee and now we boast over 3,000 members.

Six years ago, I came to Ottawa from Bangladesh, a country literally on the other side of the world, little did I know how much I would fall in love with the city. Organizing events started for very personal reasons - I just wanted to try out new things with like-minded individuals. So, I started creating various events ranging from going out to drink coffee to bungee jumping, and through these events, I have met some of the most amazing human beings, most of whom are now my close friends.

I fell in love with Ottawa because of its diversity and its amazing people. I try to give back a sense of happiness and excitement by creating events that bring people together. We also help raise funds for charitable organizations. We have helped fire victims through Red Cross, refugees through the United Nations High Commissioner for Refugees (UHNCR), and sponsored clean water initiatives in secluded parts of the continent of Africa. The increased demand for these events has led to Young & Awesome being registered as an event management company that is all encompassing in the community.

Our team still focuses on the smaller events that formed the company's roots like community-run board game nights and volleyball competitions as this allows us to strive for the future without giving up our goal. The one message I would share with everyone is to make sure you get out there and meet new people. Don't be stuck in your box, because once you open yourself to other cultures, your eyes will open up to a plethora of kindness and understanding.

If you come across an event hosted by Young & Awesome, don't hesitate to attend. We have been doing this for over five years, and we are addicted to meeting new people. Since everyone brings their own unique self to the table, it never gets boring.

Hannah Karunakar

When I was just a year old, my family and I moved to Toronto. Our apartment was run-down and I distinctly remember my mother's fear of our surroundings. But looking back, most of my memories of the city consisted of watching trains from my solarium and the reflection of headlights dance on my ceiling. I felt protected knowing that there were people just like me out there, going about their own lives. I would fall asleep feeling surrounded. With every vehicle came a different light, each acting as its own verse in a lullaby.

When I moved back to Dubai at the age of five, I found the warmth of light through streetlights, skyscrapers, offices, homes, metros, malls, and mosques. If there's a wedding or if it is Eid, you will find entire mansions lit up by majestic bulbs from top to bottom. If you manage to peek into a Sheikh's house you will find glorious chandeliers dazzling with Swarovski diamonds, reflecting upon each other. Even the mainroads have their own luminosity, covered in ads, streetlights, and car lights. Ottawa, however, was quite the change for me. When I arrived here to attend university, it did not take long for me to heed the siren call of the city lights and begin exploring my new home. I saw some light bulbs by the Rideau Canal, and it was generally populated downtown but it wasn't enough to replace the comfort of home and the absence of my family. I missed the patterns of Toronto's cars on the ceiling, or the fact that I could go out on Dubai's streets at night and feel surrounded again.

One evening in December, my friends and I decided to take on the -30 degree weather to celebrate my birthday. While exploring downtown, a chained off staircase caught my eye. In an adventurous spirit, we trudged up the stairs laden with snow, turned the corner, and were greeted by quite a site. Amongst four evenly spaced trees lay hundreds of light bulbs. Red, green, and gold lights were nestled in the branches with their warm saturate, making them look as vibrant as they appear in the summertime. Blues, purples, greens, silvers, contrasted and reflected upon each other like a kaleidoscope. Just when I thought the roof was enough, I looked below to see several dozens of lit trees below us. They guided our eyes along the shimmering Rideau Canal, igniting the pathway to see people - people just like me going about their own lives. My eyes filled with tears and my heart flickered a flame I thought was long extinguished since moving to a new city. As my frostbitten self melted away, I no longer saw the simplicity of Ottawa's lights as part of a daunting unwelcome, but an invitation to explore its secrecy. That day I found the warmth of Ottawa resting beyond a chained off staircase and hidden roof, and it was then I knew that this city would always have more for me to discover.

Sam Lehman

Photography by Felixe Denson

When I think about who I am, I automatically think of Ottawa. I was born here and I like to think that I will always return to this city. So far I haven't ventured too far from home for extended periods of time. I suppose I would like to, in fact I can confirm without a doubt that sometimes I would like to be anywhere else but here. However, there are things that keep me here and keep me grounded while my soul fights my mind to give over to my wanderlust. My status as a student is part of what reigns in my desire to get out of this town. I study the humanities at Carleton University, which means that I study everything from philosophy to literature all in relation to human culture. I read great books, I learn about the big ideas, and through it all I've become a better person. I'm more conscious of who I am and what I can do for this world. I wrote an article once about how this city breeds cynics and I think that's true, to an extent. Ottawa is also a city that cultivates compassion and kindness though. Even so, I'm a cynic at heart. I love to analyze and assess situations; I question everything. When I am not speaking, I am listening. My favourite pastime is walking by the Rideau Canal and watching people go about their lives. By watching other people I feel connected to a larger community - I feel like I belong.

THE CAPITAL'S
JE NE SAIS QUOI

Photograph provided by Zara of XO Velo

Photography by Daniel Effah

In my other job, I wrestle
In my other job, I'm stray
er job, I'm a biker
In my other job, I bless th
r job I'm a geek
In my other job, I work the r
r job, I pop up
In my other job, I curse you. R
r job, I own a lot
In my other job, I fly at yo
job, own something
In my other job, I head you
r job, I hear you
In my other job, I bear no ma
n job, I pinch who
I'd say any
job, I deliver
ear a h
er job, I u
is not
her job,
y heat
her job,
is m
r job
po
y other
woe
job I d
you
r job, I
attent
r job, I
es you
job, we decid
things
r job, I'm un
was fired
r job, I have
fixed the e
her job, I pre
hauntec
her job, I
have insur
ther job, I
lost a fi
ther job, I be
leprs
other job, I
crawl
ther job, I
vel
ther job, I
ne
ther job, I
u
my other ph
ea
my other phm
old
n my other job
fo
n my other job

I'm my other

PLEASE ALLOW ATTENDANT

TO RETRIEVE DARTS

Photography by Daniel Effah

Photography by Julia Weber

Photography by Andre Ringuette

Photography by Glen Ellis

Photography by Andre Ringuette

Photography by Landon Entwistle

Photography by Glen Ellis

Photography by Andre Ringuette

Photography by Glen Ellis

Photography by Glen Ellis

Photography by Steve Kingsman

Photography by Noorulabdeen Ahmad

Photography by John Lin

Photography by Tony Li

Photograph provided by Alt Hotel

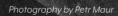
Photography by Petr Maur

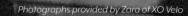

Photographs provided by House of PainT Festival

Photography by John Lin

Photography by John Lin

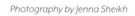

Photography by Jenna Sheikh

#WINGDOTTAWA

This hashtag aimed to encourage people on social media to share some of their favourite photographs and stories from Canada's Capital.

I moved to Ottawa-Gatineau one year ago with my kids. No friends or family here. Since then we've been exploring the area and discovering our favourite spots and activities. Hiking has become part of our daily routine. My boys love to get in the woods to spot new things, they use their imagination and together we create new stories everyday. This picture was taken on the day of Christmas Eve, and it reminds me how happy we feel in our new country.

- Fernanda Publio
(@ferpubl)

Tell me, what do you think about the view?

- Gholam Nandoko
(@golam.nandoko)

The best gift ever was her, she was a Christmas gift. I always wanted to have a dog and my parents never allowed me. My boyfriend gave her to me. So, I'm learning how to be a good dog mom. I'm committing a lot of mistakes but she is bringing me so much joy in such cold weather. I'm thankful for her.

- Milaine Astride
(@giftsandotherblunders)

This is how we shovel snow in Ottawa.

- Taba Ali
(@taba_ali)

Taking a stroll in the Experimental Farm on a sunny winter day. For once, we're gonna miss [this kind of warm] winter.

- Gregorius Erico
(@edgrer)

Ottawa is one of this country's most picturesque cities. With four beautiful seasons and some of the most amazing sunsets you'll ever see, it's easy to fall in love with Canada's Capital.

- Hannah Manning (@hannahkgm)

Spring in Ottawa.

- Sherry Zhao (@sherrylavgine1997)

Soft lights. Flowers. Lots of flowers. A friend. And of course, a camera. That's what spring looks like in Ottawa.

- Fatima Fakih
(@fatimafakih2)

Autumn is nothing short of amazing in Canada's Capital. I'm always drawn to walking by the Locks of the Rideau Canal when seasons are changing, often pausing to take a few photographs.

- Erica Giancola
(@ericagiancola)

Snowfall at the bus station.

- Thu Truong
(@sunny.tr)

This picture is a thirty second long exposure using an ND filter. I definitely enjoy this spot, it's a great area for nature pictures. When going off the trail it's best to be careful where you step so you don't slip or fall, the rocks can be slippery.

- Patrick Harris
(@pat.h.photography)

Photograph taken in Chinatown.

- Annik Lemire
(@anniklemirephotography)

A quick look around Downtown Ottawa shows a city teeming with history and those with their eyes open would be hard pressed not to catch glimpses of it around every corner. This statue, situated in Major's Hill Park, is but one example. With the ever present Parliament of Canada as a backdrop, the statue depicts a Native American gazing towards the Ottawa River, an ever important water route that was the path towards the St. Lawrence, the entrance into Canada from the sea.

- Simon Harris
(@simon.harris_photography)

There are few cities in the world where you can portage a canoe and go for a paddle in the middle of downtown for your lunch break. Ottawa represents for me an amazing city for a work life balance with nature. Within minutes of downtown, you can glide along the longest skating surface in the world, hike in a world class park, paddle the historic Rideau Canal, launch yourself down ski mountain or snowshoe to a secluded yurt.

- Nathan Skolski
(@nathanocracy)

Liam Spero captured this photo at our Summer Fiesta event. At Eephorea, we deliver fun times to awesome people! We don't just host events, we create memorable experiences. Our interactive activities are simply unforgettable. Let's celebrate together! All are welcomed, none are judged. Welcome to our world. Welcome to Eephorea!

- Zach Princi
(@eephorea)

This photo was captured by Dunica Shamoy at my Spring 2017 preview party which was held on December 22, 2016 at the Alt Hotel in Ottawa. This photo is everything to me, it depicts cultural diversity, inclusiveness, growth, and achievement.

- King B. Hector Jr.
(@_wearekings)

This monument is a commemorative work of public art, gifted by the Republic of Turkey. It is dedicated to all public servants and diplomats in foreign service who have fallen while serving their country. It is located at the intersection of Island Park Drive and Sir John A. Macdonald Parkway in Ottawa. Its large open face is directed toward the "gateway of eternity," while its smaller extremity points toward the earth, opening into the "gateway of time." In the shape of a sphere, this monument symbolizes the eternal resting place of the fallen. The metal prisms inside represent those who have made the ultimate sacrifice. The single prism located at the "gateway of time" pays special tribute to Colonel Altıkat, military attaché of the Embassy of the Republic of Turkey in Ottawa, who was assassinated on August 27, 1982, close to where the monument is located.

This commemorative work of public art was created by artists, Azimet Karaman, sculptor; Levent Timurhan, architect; Reha Benderlioğlu, architect-sculptor; and Necmettin Yağcı, sculptor.

- Turkish Embassy
(@turkishembassyinottawa)

I find that this is a city with a simple elegance.

- Alek Tirpan
(@tirp_a)

HEREAFTER

Provided by the National Capital Commission /
Commission de la capitale nationale (NCC/CCN)

The Capital represents the heart of Canada's democracy. As a symbol of our history, heritage and culture, it embodies the Canadian character and spirit - our rich history, our vibrant present, and our aspirations for the future.

The National Capital Commission (NCC) is the federal Crown Corporation dedicated to ensuring that Canada's Capital is a source of pride for all Canadians, and a source of inspiration for generations to come. It does this by fulfilling three roles: Planner (maintaining and executing a long-term vision for federal lands in the Capital); Steward (protecting and preserving our nationally significant public places); Partner (working with others to encourage and ensure excellence in both development and conservation).

The diverse and dynamic Capital we are building today is the Capital our young people will inherit tomorrow - which is why it is so vital that they take an active role in defining what it is, and what it can be. The needs of the Capital and Canadians are constantly evolving, and the NCC's planning framework must do the same. The Commission is currently finalizing the latest Plan for Canada's Capital, which will chart a course for the Capital Region over the next fifty years - from 2017 to 2067, the bicentennial of Canada's Confederation.

The Plan for Canada's Capital, 2017 to 2067, will build on a rich legacy of Capital planning stretching back more than a century. Under its three guiding themes we will continue building an inspiring capital, a capital that is inclusive, meaningful, picturesque, natural, thriving and connected.

Between 2017 and the Bicentennial, a series of major milestone projects will transform the Capital on both sides of the Ottawa River:

· An Indigenous welcome centre on Victoria Island.

· Significant new commemorative sites, including a celebration of the Canadian Charter of Rights and Freedoms.

· New national institutions, including a National Portrait Gallery, a National Botanical Garden, and a science and innovation centre.

· The renewal of 24 Sussex Drive, the official residence of the Prime Minister of Canada.

· The creation of the Capital Illumination Plan to enhance the Capital's beauty at night.

· Improvements to the Capital's shorelines and green spaces.

· The redevelopment of LeBreton Flats and Chaudière and Albert Islands.

· Renewed views protection to preserve the place of our national symbols in the Capital's skyline.

· Improvements to the integration of federal employment areas.

· Improvements to the interface between the Capital realm and the civic realm on Confederation Boulevard and the connections leading to it.

· Improvements to interprovincial transportation and the integration of public transit systems and inter-modal links.

· The rejuvenation of Nepean Point and completion of the shoreline parkway from the Rideau Canal to Rideau Falls.

· The regeneration of the Capital's urban forest.

· The protection of ecological corridors and our natural heritage.

· Improvements to trails and the creation of a new visitor centre in Gatineau Park.

· The revitalization of Gatineau's Ruisseau de la Brasserie (Brewery Creek) sector.

· The completion of the Greenbelt Pathway network.

AFTERWORD

Ottawa is an exciting, beautiful and vibrant city. As Minister of Small Business and Tourism, I've had the chance to meet many amazing entrepreneurs in this city.

This guidebook provides an insider's view of many things that make Ottawa so great. Whether you're a first time visitor or you're a born and bred Ottawan, this city offers countless opportunities for adventure. From biking on the extensive National Capital Commission pathways or paddling down the Canal or the rivers, to taking part in one of the many annual festivals or events, this city really has something for everyone.

There are many small and medium-sized enterprises (SMEs) that are an important part of the Capital's landscape. Not only do businesses in Ottawa make the city a more dynamic place, they also contribute to the country's economy in a significant way. Ottawa is home to many top technology companies that play a key role in making Canada a nation of innovators. In the past five years, these companies have raised more money in the public markets than all other Canadian cities combined!

I launched the Millennial Travel Program and the #farandaway hashtag in anticipation of Canada's 150th anniversary. This program encourages millennials to connect with and explore their country, and to become lifetime ambassadors for Canada both at home and abroad. Whether you attend one of the many music festivals in Ottawa, do yoga on Parliament Hill, go whitewater rafting, or discover new dishes, show us and use #farandaway.

It is thanks to groups like the Wingd team who put this guidebook together that visitors come from all over the world to discover what this city has to offer. This book will surely encourage locals and tourists to explore Ottawa.

Minister of Small Business and Tourism, Honourable Bardish Chagger.
Photograph provided by the office of the Minister of Small Business and Tourism

ACKNOWLEDGEMENTS

The Wingd Team would like to acknowledge:

The entire community of Ottawa for supporting us and making our dream of creating a book come true by encouraging us with your words, advice and loyalty to our craft. We sincerely thank you for getting us to where we are today.

Donors to our book - thank you to Claire Leunissen, Kenneth Lehman, Philippe-Olivier Giroux, and our partners at Advanced Dermatology for helping us make our first print project materialize.

Mayor Jim Watson for inviting us to your office to discuss our book and our vision for it. Thank you sincerely for taking the time out of your busy schedule to listen to us.

Minister of Small Business and Tourism, Honourable Bardish Chagger, for supporting our book and writing its afterword.

Premier of Ontario, Honourable Kathleen Wynne, for sending us a congratulatory message wishing us success on our book and for encouraging our efforts.

National Capital Commission / Commission de la capitale nationale (NCC/CCN), Ottawa Tourism and Ottawa 2017 for being our friends and partners, and for offering advice and for contributing pertinent information to our book.

The entire media team in Ottawa that has supported us along the way. Partners include Metro Ottawa, Ottawa Citizen, Ottawa Sun, Apt613, University of Ottawa's Fulcrum Newspaper, Daytime Ottawa, CHUO 89.1 FM, and Carleton University's CKCU-FM.

Our social media community, specifically those on our Instagram account (@wingd.ca). Thank you for contributing all the photos you did with #wingdottawa. Please continue to engage with us and we look forward to future collaborations.

Thank you to every photographer who is not affiliated with Wingd but contributed to our book.

Thank you to our printers and publishers over at Baico Publishing Consultants Inc. and Du Progrès Printing for helping us make our dream come true with this book and for standing by us over the past two years.

Thank you to all our friends and family for their love, support and guidance every step of the way.

CONTRIBUTORS

Zainab N. Muse
Editor & Creator

David Ebere
Creator

Sam Lehman
Editor & Writer

Gloria Charles-Pierre
Writer & Translator

Julia Weber
Writer & Photographer

Felixe Denson
Writer & Photographer

Richard E. Gower
Writer

Navita Patel
Writer

Lorietta Muse
Writer

Claire Leunissen
Writer

Sarah Khalid
Writer

Soumi Ghosh
Writer

Shuyi Yang
Photo Editor

Daniel Effah
Photographer

Rebecca Hay
Photographer

Jenna Sheikh
Photographer

Tony Li
Photographer

Syed Zeehad
Photographer

John (Finnigan) Lin
Photographer

Noorulabdeen Ahmad
Photographer

Jimmy Lau
Marketing Intern

Paroma Datta
Publicist

Rachelle Bélanger
Contributor

Boris Nzaramba
Contributor

Orphane Beaulière
Contributor

Amulya Gururaj
Contributor

Anjali Ramburn
Contributor

Michael Tang
Contributor

APPENDIX [A]

Additional details on events and locations mentioned in the book

Aberdeen Pavilion
Located at 1000 Exhibition Way in Ottawa, Ontario.

Alexandra Bridge
A bridge that connects the cities of Ottawa and Gatineau.

Andrew Haydon Park
Located at 3169 Carling Avenue in Nepean, Ontario.

Arboretum Festival
An annual music festival that takes place in Ottawa, Ontario. For more information, visit:
www.arboretumfestival.com

Art Battle
An all year round live painting competition. For more information, visit: www.artbattle.com/category/ottawa

Breton Beach
Located within the Gatineau Park.

Britannia Park
Located at Britannia Bay. Address: 2805 Carling Avenue, Ottawa.

Bytown Museum
Located at 1 Canal Lane in Ottawa, Ontario. For more information, visit: www.bytownmuseum.com

Byward Market
One of Canada's oldest public markets established in 1826.

Calabogie Peaks Resort (Eagle's Nest Lookout)
Located at 30 Barrett Chute Road in Calabogie, Ontario.

Camp Fortune
Located at 300 Chemin Dunlop in Chelsea, Quebec. For more information, visit:
www.campfortune.com

Canada Day
A federal statutory holiday that occurs on the 1st of July every year across Canada.

Canadian Children's Museum
Located at 100 Rue Laurier in Gatineau, Quebec. For more information, visit:
www.historymuseum.ca/visit/childrens-museum

Canadian Museum of History
Located at 100 Rue Laurier in Gatineau, Quebec. For more information, visit:
www.historymuseum.ca

Canadian Museum of Nature
Located at 240 McLeod Street in Ottawa, Ontario. For more information, visit: www.nature.ca

Canadian Tulip Festival
An annual festival that occurs across Canada. For more information, visit:
www.tulipfestival.ca

Canadian War Museum
Located at 1 Vimy Place in Ottawa, Ontario. For more information, visit: www.warmuseum.ca

Cardinal Creek Karst
Located at 1056 Watters Road in Orléans, Ontario.

Casino du Lac-Leamy Sound of Light
An annual international fireworks competition. For more information, visit:
www.feux.qc.ca/home

Changing of the Guard
An annual summer tradition in Ottawa, Ontario that began in 1959.

Chinatown
An area that is home to businesses from many Asian cultures. For more information, visit:
www.ottawachinatown.ca

Christmas Lights Across Canada
An annual winter program that takes place in the Capital Region.

Corktown Footbridge
A bridge that connects Somerset Street East in Sandy Hill and the University of Ottawa with Somerset Street West in Centretown in Ottawa, Ontario.

Diefenbunker Museum
Located at 3929 Carp Road in Carp, Ontario. For more information, visit:
www.diefenbunker.ca

Dow's Lake
Located at 1001 Queen Elizabeth Drive in Ottawa, Ontario. For more information, visit:
www.dowslake.com

Dunbar Bridge
The Bronson Overpass. Located at 100 Brewer Way in Ottawa, Ontario.

Elgin Street
One of the busiest streets located in Downtown Ottawa, Ontario.

Escapade Eskimo
An outdoor adventure company. Located at 1378 Route 301 in Otter Lake, Quebec. For more information, visit: www.escapade-eskimo.com

Escape Manor
Located at 201 Queen Street in Ottawa, Ontario. For more information, visit: www.escapemanor.com

Fairmont Château Laurier
Located at 1 Rideau Street in Ottawa, Ontario. For more information, visit: www.fairmont.com/laurier-ottawa

Gatineau Loppet
An annual cross-country ski race. For more information, visit: www.gatineauloppet.com

Gatineau Park
Located at 33 Scott Road in Chelsea, Quebec. For more information, visit:www.ncc-ccn. gc.ca/places-to-visit/gatineau-park

Glowfair
An annual festival that takes place on Bank Street in Ottawa, Ontario. For more information, visit: www.glowfairfestival.ca

Great Canadian Bungee
An outdoor adventure company. Located at 1780 Route 105 in Wakefield, Quebec. For more information, visit: www.bungee.ca

Great Glebe Garage Sale
An annual outdoor sale event that takes place in the Glebe neighbourhood in Ottawa, Ontario.

Haunted Walk of Ottawa
Located at 46 Sparks Street in Ottawa, Ontario. For more information, visit: www.hauntedwalk.com

HI-Ottawa Jail Hostel
Located at 75 Nicholas Street in Ottawa, Ontario. For more information, visit: www.hihostels.ca/ Ontario/1166/HI-Ottawa-Jail.hostel

Hintonburg
A neighbourhood located west of Downtown Ottawa, Ontario.

Hog's Back Falls
Located at Hog's Back Road in Ottawa, Ontario. For more information, visit: www.ncc-ccn. gc.ca/places-to-visit/parks-paths/ hog's-back-park

HOPE Volleyball Summerfest
HOPE (Helping Other People Everywhere) is an annual charity event that takes place in Ottawa, Ontario. For more information, visit: www.hopehelps.com

House of PainT Festival
An annual event that began in Ottawa, Ontario in 2003. For more information, visit: www.houseofpaint.ca

Jacques-Cartier Park
Located on Laurier Street in Gatineau, Quebec. For more information, visit: www.ncc-ccn. gc.ca/places-to-visit/parks-paths/ jacques-cartier-park

Jitsu Ottawa
A community club offering martial arts classes. Located at 155 Loretta Avenue North and in Carleton Univeristy in Ottawa, Ontario. For more information, visit: www.jitsuottawa.com

Lansdowne Park
Located at 450 Queen Elizabeth Drive in Ottawa, Ontario.

Leamy Lake Park
Located in Gatineau, Quebec. For more information, visit: www. ncc-ccn.gc.ca/places-to-visit/parks-paths/leamy-lake-park

Lord Elgin Hotel
Located at 100 Elgin Street in Ottawa, Ontario. For more information, visit: www.lordelginhotel.ca

Lusk Cave
Located on Trail 54 in Sainte-Cécile-de-Masham, Quebec. For more information, visit: www.ncc-ccn.gc. ca/places-to-visit/gatineau-park/ lusk-cave

Major's Hill Park
Located on Mackenzie Avenue in Ottawa, Ontario. For more information, visit: www.ncc-ccn. gc.ca/places-to-visit/parks-paths/ majors-hill-park

Meech Lake
Located within the Gatineau Park.

Mer Bleue Conservation Area
Located on Ridge Road in Ottawa, Ontario. For more information, visit: www.ncc-ccn.gc.ca/places-to-visit/ greenbelt/mer-bleue

Mooney's Bay Park
Located at 2960 Riverside Drive in Ottawa, Ontario.

Morrison's Quarry
Located in Wakefield, Quebec.

National Arts Centre (NAC)
Located at 53 Elgin Street in Ottawa, Ontario. For more information, visit: www.nac-cna.ca

National Gallery of Canada
Located at 380 Sussex Drive in
Ottawa, Ontario. For more
information, visit: www.gallery.ca

National War Memorial
Designed by Vernon March.
Located on Wellington Street in
Downtown Ottawa, Ontario.

Nepean Point
A hill located behind the National
Gallery of Canada at 380 Sussex
Drive in Ottawa, Ontario.

Notre-Dame Cathedral Basilica
Located at 385 Sussex Drive in
Ottawa, Ontario. For more
information, visit:
www.notredameottawa.com

Nuit Blanche
An annual event that takes place at
multiple locations across the
Capital Region. For more
information, visit: www.nbog.ca

Ottawa's RBC Bluesfest Festival
An outdoor music festival that
takes place every summer in
Ottawa, Ontario. For more
information, visit:
www.ottawabluesfest.ca

Ottawa River
One of the most historic rivers in
Canada that connects the
provinces of Ontario and Quebec.

Parliament Hill
Located on Wellington Street in
Downtown Ottawa, Ontario.

Pink Lake
Located within Gatineau Park

Preston Street
This street is affectionately known
as "Little Italy" and is one of the
busiest streets in Ottawa, Ontario.

Prince of Wales Bridge
A now defunct rail bridge that
connected the cities of Ottawa and
Gatineau.

Princess Louise Falls
Located on St. Joseph Boulevard in
Ottawa, Ontario.

Remic Rapids Park
Located on Sir John A. Macdonald
Parkway in Ottawa, Ontario.

Rideau Canal
A waterway that was built in 1832
and that connects the cities of
Kingston and Ottawa in Ontario. It
is about 202 km in total length.

Rideau Falls
Located at 1 Sussex Drive in
Ottawa, Ontario.

Saunders Farm
Located at 7893 Bleeks Rd in
Ottawa, Ontario. For further
information, visit:
www.saundersfarm.com

Shirleys Bay
Located at about 10 miles West of
Ottawa. For more information, visit:
www.ncc-ccn.gc.ca/places-to-visit/
greenbelt/shirleys-bay

Sound and Light Show
A bilingual show presented nightly
on Parliament Hill. It typically runs
from the months of July to
September every year.

Sparks Street
One of the oldest pedestrian streets
that was established in Ottawa,
Ontario in 1967.

Supreme Court of Canada
Located at 301 Wellington Street in
Ottawa, Ontario. For more
information, visit: www.scc-csc.ca

Tim Hortons Ottawa Dragon Boat
Festival
A multi-day festival adapted from
historic Chinese traditions. For more
information, visit:
www.dragonboat.net

Whitewater Rafting
A suggested company to contact is
Wilderness Tours Adventure Resort
at www.wildernesstours.com

Winterlude Festival
An annual winter festival that takes
place around the Capital Region.

Urban Fly Co.
A fly fishing company based in
Ottawa, Ontario. For more
information, visit:
www.urbanflycodotcom.wordpress.
com

Yoga on Parliament Hill
An annual program run on the
lawn of Parliament Hill to foster
yoga practices across the Capital.

APPENDIX [B]

Additional details on some of the people mentioned in the book

Alfonso Abizaid
For more information, visit:
www.carleton.ca/neuroscience/
people/alfonso-abizaid

Allan André
For more information, visit:
www.allanandre.com

Alyssa Spaxman
For more information, visit:
www.strutjewelry.com

Amanda Parriag
For more information, visit:
www.media-action-media.com

Bardish Chagger
For more information, visit:
www.pm.gc.ca/minister/
honourable-bardish-chagger

Chantal Sarkisian
For more information, visit:
www.modexlusive.com

Corey Sheikh and Michael Alemao
For more information, visit:
www.umtbc.com

Eric Koch and Will Porter
For more information, visit:
www.lunchboxottawa.com

Grace Lam
For more information, visit:
www.graceesthetics.com

Jaime Koebel
For more information, visit:
www.indigenouswalks.com

Jamie Pistilli
For more information, visit: www.
urbanflycodotcom.wordpress.com

Jasmine Mah and Catherine Zadeh
For more information, visit:
www.ottawapolefitness.com

Jessica Vermette and Jenna Hutcheson
For more information, visit:
www.ottawamakersmarket.com

Jim Watson
For more information, visit:
www.jimwatsonottawa.ca

Judy-Hum Delaney
For more information, visit:
www.ottawafoodiegirlz.com

Julie Beun
For more information, visit:
www.jbeun.media

Katie Hession
For more information, visit:
www.yowcitystyle.tumblr.com

Kimani Peter
For more information, visit:
www.citizensofonyx.com

King B. Hector Jr.
For more information, visit:
www.wearekings.ca

Lynn Jatania
For more information, visit:
www.blogoutloud.org

Mark O'Neill
For more information, visit:
www.historymuseum.ca

Michael Crockatt
For more information, visit:
www.ottawatourism.ca

Nabil Imani
For more information, visit:
www.youngandawesome.ca

Nina Kressler
For more information, visit:
www.shaw-centre.com

Noel Paine
For more information, visit:
www.noelpaine.wordpress.com

Rachel Décoste
For more information, visit:
www.racheldecoste.ca

Raymond Lin, Leon Li and Yuanchen Zhu
For more information, visit:
www.ottawazine.com

Rob Spittall
For more information, visit:
www.thecomicbookshoppe.com

Sam Turgeon-Brabazon
For more information, visit:
www.samsprouts.com

Saveeta Sharma
For more information, visit:
www.upasana.ca

Tammy Giuliani
For more information, visit:
www.slgelato.com

Vaughn MacDonald, Alexandra Ekstrom and Steven Yong
For more information, visit:
www.blacksquirrelbooks.ca

Zara of XO Velo
For more information, visit:
www.xovelo.com

Statistics, dates, and facts about the Capital listed in this book were provided by our friends and supporters at Ottawa Tourism and the National Capital Commission / Commission de la capitale nationale (NCC/CCN).

CONTACT WINGD

www.wingd.ca

info@wingd.ca

Connect with us on Social media

Facebook: Wingd.ca

Twitter: @wingdcanada

Instagram: @wingd.ca